Randigal Rhymes, and a Glossary of Cornish Words

PREFACE.

———

IN accordance with the expressed desire of many gentlemen of the neighbourhood, friends of our father, who were most anxious that his Verses and collection of Cornish Dialect Words should be given to the public, we have put together such of his works as we think may be generally useful and interesting. Himself a Cornishman, he took the greatest interest in the Dialect of his native County, specially that of West Cornwall, with which he was most familiar, having lived there for the greater part of his life.

It was always his regret, that with the opening up of the County, and a greater intercourse with other peoples, the expressive phrases and peculiar words of Cornwall should fast give place to forms of speech less forcible and interesting. The Glossary only includes words, expressions, etc., which our father himself has personally met with and heard used. The collection was begun some thirty years ago, when a short residence at Liskeard enabled him to get an insight of the Dialect of the East of Cornwall. The occasional jotting down of a word when met with, often without its definition, has made the work of the compilers most difficult, and possibly does not do the author justice.

PREFACE.

The Rhymes are the work of spare moments, and were written chiefly for the amusement of his friends, and also with the object, as far as possible, of preserving the nearly disused dialect. Several of these pieces have, from time to time, appeared in local publications under the *nom de plume* of "Imspriven" They were received so favourably that we venture to hope their re-issue, with the others included in this little book, will conduce to an extensive circulation, and be a source of interest and amusement where Cornish people gather

Finally, we beg to thank all who have subscribed, for their valuable assistance to the publication of this, very Cornish, book.

G. & W. H. THOMAS

St Michael's Mount,
    January, 1895.

Memoir.

Mr Joseph Thomas, the Author of the "Dialect Poems" contained in the following pages, now first gathered and published as a labour of love by his children, was born at Clahar Garden, in the Parish of Mullion, Cornwall, on July 28th, 1840 His father, Mr. John Thomas, was for many years the local Steward for Lord Robartes, and was, like his gifted son, fond of and familiar with the Antiquities of the County and neighbourhood, which, with his ample store of legendary lore, coupled with the inferences drawn and his observations of the people and places, contributed to his opinion being sought by Mr. W. C. Borlase and other antiquarians.

Mr. Joseph Thomas was educated at the late Mr Robert Blight's school, at Penzance. and being intended to adopt his father's profession of Land Agent and Valuer, he entered the office of Mr Sylvanus Jenkin, at Liskeard, for the purpose of studying Land Surveying, &c , remaining from 1866 to 1868, whence he removed to St Michael's Mount in September, 1868—Sir Edward St. Aubyn having engaged him as Assistant Agent to Mr Edward St Aubyn, in which capacity he gained such a confidential position that a great deal of the management of the estates was left in his hands of late years—an issue fulfilling the expectation of his senior friends, who, knowing the stock from which he descended, reckoned on the descent also of their intelligence and mental qualities.

In March, 1869, he was married to Mary, only daughter of William and Mary Hendy, of Bonython, Cury.

He had a most prepossessing appearance—tall, manly, handsome.

He was a wide reader, an able controversialist, and being also of high Christian character, joined to great information and talent for communicating it, he was an acceptable preacher. For four or five generations his family had been preachers. Among those of his family may be enumerated his two brothers, four uncles, two grandfathers, his grandmother's brother, his uncle's grandfather, and his great grandfather—the latter probably being a preacher in Wesley's days—a continuous chain of preachers, unique even in the annals of Cornish families, and he himself, as mentioned, was popular as a preacher among United Methodist Free Church congregations.

Possessing great geniality of disposition, he was inflexible for whatever he believed to be the right. In Theology he stood in the old paths of Methodism, and grieved over the departure from those paths of many who occupy its pulpits. Nor had he much sympathy with some modern methods of attracting men to the House of God. His loss to the church of his choice seems simply irreparable. He held the offices of Circuit Steward, Local Preacher, Class Leader, and Trustee His influence in official meetings was always good. He followed the things which make for peace Those that knew him best loved him most.

A local issue remarks :—" Had Mr. Thomas devoted more time to literature he would have made his mark in portraying Cornish dialect, with which, and its quaint stories and incidents, he was so familiar." Mr. Thomas obtained his materials at first hand by chatting with all sorts and conditions of men and women, in a homely and friendly way, that elicited superstitions, droll fancies, and curious reminiscences.

Mr. Thomas was always of a studious disposition, and made good use of the library of his parents, and intercourse with intelligent friends. When the " Lady Elizabeth " Hall at Porthgwarra was opened, a year or two ago, he spoke of the extraordinary opportunities young people now have of acquiring knowledge, compared with that of lads, like himself, in remote country places 30 or 35 years ago. His own example showed how greatly he appreciated the value and pleasure of wide reading.

His social qualities and conversational powers made his company highly entertaining, and he took general interest in all phases of life At a recent Corpus Christi Fair at Penzance, he chatted with the writer on the lives of the Show People. He said " it used to be a regular custom for them to visit St Michael's Mount during their stay at Penzance," and of some of them he had then learned of the roughness, yet fascinating variety, and freedom of the life from which they could not separate themselves. So, from itinerant showmen, as well as from Cornish miners, farm labourers, fishermen, and others, he gleaned interesting facts and obtained glimpses of life. At the Fair he seemed to be in the best of health and spirits,—yet within a few weeks the active mind had ceased to move in its earthly tenement, and we have to deplore the death of an esteemed friend, and sympathise with a sorrowing family. His death was, humanly speaking, premature. His complaint was pneumonia, but there were further developments. He received the most skilful medical attention, and was nursed with the most affectionate zeal, but, despite all efforts, he sank, and on Wednesday, 13th June, 1894, he entered into rest. His Father and God had need of him and took him home. He left a widow and large family to mourn his death.

His interment took place on Saturday, the 16th June, in the parish cemetery belonging to Lord St. Levan, in which those who die at St. Michael's Mount are usually interred It took place in the presence of a large gathering of deeply affected friends, — and during the ceremony an incident occurred which attracted the attention of many present : a pair of doves, which Mr. Thomas had presented to Lord St. Levan's youngest son, and were caged at the Castle, escaped just at the hour, and taking flight, alighted in the tree just over the grave, where they remained spectators of the mournful proceeding, apparently unaffected by the concourse.

The Scripture assure us that—" The things which are seen are temporal, the things which are not seen are eternal, ... we know that if our earthly house of this tabernacle were dissolved we have a building of God," and this knowledge formed the stay of, and was the abiding rest of, our dear friend's soul—ever and anon finding expression in words as shown in the following stanzas, which were the last work of the Author.—

A FRAGMENT

*　　　*　　　*　　　*

AND we have wandered, sad at heart, and weary,
　The sunlight gone, forsaken, in distress,
And all the prospect seemed to us a dreary,
　Vast, friendless, solitary wilderness,
Until the heavenly vision o er us stealing.—
　The stony pillow, and the desert sod
Became to our awed souls, by His revealing,
　The Gate of Heaven, and the House of God.

How often, in the hopelessness of grief,
　We wander forth, the sepulchre to see,
And, in the blindness of our unbelief,
　Have yielded to the grave the victory,—
Until One standing near has gently bidden
　Us " be of comfort," and at that sweet word
We've turned to witness what our tears have hidden—
　The gracious presence of our risen Lord

His Royal Highness Prince Albrecht of Prussia, Regent of Brunswick, and suite, visited St Michael's Mount in April, 1892 And His Royal Highness having again visited the Mount in May, 1895. kindly inquired after the genial steward, Mr. Thomas, and when told he was dead, expressed his regret The party ultimately visited the cemetery, and when shewn, at the special request of the Prince, Mr. Thomas's grave, one of the gentlemen remarked, " We shall meet again."

THOMAS   LEAN.

The " Gew,"
        Marazion.

CONTENTS.

———

For aw would minchey, play at feaps, or prall a dog or cat,
Or strub a nest, unhang a gate, or anything like that."
Just then Great Jem stroathed down the lane, and shouted
        out so bold :
" You're like the Ruan Vean men, soase, ' don't knaw and
        waant be told ' ; " *
Aw staved right in amongst them, and aw fetched that boy
        a clout,
Just down below the nuddick, and aw scat the bully out ;
That there's the boy that's standing where the keggas are
        in blowth :
Blest ! if aw haven't got another bully in his mouth ! "

————

I CLIMBED the hill, and by a rustic stile,
    Where oft at eve the village lovers meet,
I lay me down to rest, and watched awhile
    The shadow-waves pass o'er the bending wheat,
Across whose leafy surface breezes made
    Their paths, and lightly passed with errant pace,
Shade chasing sunlight, sunlight chasing shade,
    Like smiles and frowns on Beauty's fitful face,
    Where constancy might seek in vain a resting place.

The sound of scythe-stone o'er the ringing blade
    Came from the scented fields of falling hay,
Blent with the cheerful song of village maid,
    Who 'cross the meadows blithely took her way,

---

* Local proverb.

To where the sad-eyed cows stood, near the gate,
  And waited for the welcome summons home;
The vagrant cuckoo called his answering mate,
  As he from hedge to hedge did idly roam,
  Or crossed with wayward flight yon mountain's **rugged**
    dome.

With gentle echoes of the rustling chime
  Of heather-bells, the breeze came o'er the stile,
Bearing sweet odours of the purple thyme,
  Of yellow furze, and scented camomile.
It was the early evening hour, when soon
  The day's long task of labour would be done;
Far in the purple east the patient moon,
  Pale as a cloud, her journey just begun,
  Waited the slow departure of the lingering sun.

With scythe on shoulder, from the falling swath
  A mower came, with labour-weighted feet,
And slowly trudged along the rugged path,
  And at the stile a comrade chanced to meet:
Their greetings o'er, upon the bank they sat,
  And idly stretched their weary limbs, and fell
Into the quiet luxury of chat,
  And smoked the seasoned pipes they loved so well,
  While one unto his mate this simple tale did tell.

THE MOWER'S TALE.

" I'll tell ee what 'twas all about, soase: down there, in the
    lewth of the Cairn,
I had a little small quellat, aw twadden much more than
    a garne,

When I took en aw was in barley arish ; you never, in all
    your born days,
Seed such a shape as was left there by that old Nickey
    Keskeys,
For the hedges was nothing but gurgeys, and the linhay
    had lost all its slate ;
One shevver, the hangbow, and millyer, was all that was
    left of the gate ;
The brembles growed over the voyers, the cundards was all
    left to chuck ;
And the land it was boiling weth dralyers, mores, pilf, and
    all sorts of muck ;
I've a nice little blog of a hoss, aw have got a great droke
    in his cheens,
I boft en at Goldsinney Feer,—aw es now getting up in his
    teens.
So I ploughed, and I scuffled, and harvey'd, and I raked
    all the pilf off the land,
Till I got en as plum as a want-pile, and I haaled home
    some oar-weed and sand ;
I bought some mun down to the Cove, about thirty gurries
    or more,
And I scud the whole over the land, 'twas a brave suant
    flue to be sure ;
I teel'd all the voyers to taties, and to pellas I sowed a
    brave splat ;
And I had twenty lases of baga-roots, or it might have
    been better than that.
Billy Guy, he had an old sow, some slips, and a bosom of
    veers,—

They were thurl as a passel of greyhounds, and as wild and
    as breachy as deers,

And the way they went straking and scramming would tire
    the patience of man,

Like cousin Ann Harry's old gander, " they always were on
    the ran-dan," *

And he woulden ring them, nor span them, and most of the
    time they were found

In my little quellat a-muzzling, and stanking things out of
    the ground.

So one day I went down long and told 'n if he wudden
    keep them pigs back

I would break their old gamberns, or shut them, and he
    never said gick nor gack,

But his wife came out, swayging her hands, and said :
    " Here's a brave how-dy-do

'Bout a few old taties and turmuts,—they are a nawble
    nack too,—

They are nothing but rubbage and scroff ; a wes lot of trade
    you can't see ,

So take and go the west home, and dos'en aw come anist
    me."

Now Billy aw tried to keep cooram, but aw cudden do
    nothing with she,

For she called me a scrovey great bussa, and 'bused and
    ballyragged me ;

So I told her all I knowed about her, and I squinneyed my
    eyes, and I glazed,

* Local proverb

And I skrinked up my nose just like she do, and I drove
    her downright ramping mazed ;
She catched up a cherk, and she strammed at my head, and
    jest scat in the bones ;
Then she coosed me half way up the hill, throwing bullies,
    and tubbans, and stones.
Next day I found down in the quellat three slips and an old
    spotted sow ;
So I throwed down a kayer of huddicks, and slocked them
    all into my crow,
And when I had slammed home the door, I called to that
    youngster of Jan's,
And we caggled them over with tar, and pralled them with
    old lattace pans ;
They went, as they tore down the lane, a bra coose, as you
    may suppose,
Till they met with Billy Guy's wife, a-carring a flasket of
    clothes ;
Them pigs, they ran right 'tween her legs, and they turned
    her a crickmole complete,—
They throwed her a regular qualker, and scud the clothes
    all round the street,
And the pigs, and the pans, and the clothes, the flasket and
    Billy Guy's wife,
They got tangled up altogether,—you never seed such a
    shine in your life,
For they squarded her garments to fletters—some skeats
    they would measure a yard ;
And you'd scat your sides laughing to see how suently she
    was gas-tarred.

F'rall they tried for to find out who done it, they never
    could prove it was me,

But, like Sammy said for the leaven, they'd ' a jealous thoft
    of en,' * you see.

That's more than twelve months ago , sence then, there is
    what you may call

A corisy-like between us, and they waant speak to me
    at all.

But sence they have found out for certain that I'd stand no
    more of their rigs

I've had no more trouble nor bother on account of their
    breachy old pigs."

I LINGERED till the moon that night
Threw a long track of shimmering light
Across the silent bay,
Where one lone bark, with idle sail,
Clear outlined in the moonbeams pale,
Scarce drifted on her way.

---

* Sammy T—— was a South of Helston man. Having business
in Falmouth early one morning, he dressed before day, took his
dinner-bag, and went into the pantry in the dark and fetched his
dinner. After finishing his business in Falmouth, he met a friend
in the street, and proposed that they should share a good pasty
which he had in his-pocket. They entered an inn, ordered some
beer and plates, knives and forks; when these were brought,
Sammy untied the bag, took it by the bottom corners, and shook
out——the leaven ! Sammy looked at it in blank amazement for a
time, then shook his head and said : "Ah ! I always had a jealous
thoft of en "

With buoyant heart and step I strode
Gaily along the homeward road,
　　Which echoed to my tread.
Now meeting some belated wight,
Who passed me with a frank " Good night,'
　　And cheerful nod of head.

With lingering steps a loving pair,—
A sturdy youth, a maiden fair,
　　With timid, downcast eye,
And guardian arm securely placed
Around an unresisting waist,
　　Went fondly whispering by.

The faithful hound that watched the farm,
Roused by my step, barked his alarm,
　　As I the lane passed through,
While in the vale, where tall elms stood,
The lone owl woke the echoing wood
　　With his weird " te-whit-to-whoo ! "

Then turning sharply down the hill
I paused awhile, where the old mill
　　Ground out the snowy meal,
And watched where, in the pale moonlight,
The rushing waters, foaming white,
　　Dashed o'er the mossy wheel.

Then o'er the downs, where, by the way,
On a rude mound of stone and clay,
　　A miner stout and strong

Stood in rough garments, soiled and brown,
And, as the skip wound up and down,
   He sung this lusty song.

SONG.

Come all ye jolly tinners who
   To Camborne Town belong,
Sit down and touch your pipe, my dears,
   And listen to my song :
Hundards of fitty looking maids
   In Camborne you may see,
But little Kitty Cornish is
   The crop of the bunch to me.

I saw her as I came from bal,
   Her gook, I caant tell how,
Fell back upon her nuddick, and
   The sun shone on her brow ;
Her cruddly hair was plethoned up,
   So beautiful to see,
And little Kitty Cornish is
   The crop of the bunch to me.

Her smile was bright as May, her cheeks
   Had caught the rose's hue,
Her eyes were blue as guckoo flowers,
   And sparkled like the dew ;
Her lips were red as hagglans,
   Full ripe upon the tree,
And little Kitty Cornish is
   The crop of the bunch to me.

I called—she had her towser on,
    A-mooling of the bread—
And as she put the dough to plum
    This here is what I said :
" I'd like some of that fuggan, dear,
    If I may stay to tea ; "
And little Kitty Cornish is
    The crop of the bunch to me.

I've heard the lark sing in the sky,
    The greybird in the brake,
I've heard the choir at " Wesley "
    (That's grand, and no mistake),
But sweeter far her whisper when
    She promised for to be
My own dear Kitty Cornish, and
    The crop of the bunch to me.

'Tis sweet to feel the sunshine as
    You come from underground,
'Tis sweet to breathe the fresh, fresh air,
    And see the flowers around,
But sweeter than the sunlight,
    Or honey from the bee,
Is my own dear Kitty Cornish,
    The crop of the bunch to me.

The Quest of the Gwidgy-gwee.

A SAGE Professor came into the west,
   From Oxford Town came he,
A man of fame, with a tail to his name
   Of M.A., LL.D.

He sought, 'mongst things that creep on land,
   'Mongst things that fly in air,
'Mongst things that be in the deep salt sea,
   All creatures strange and rare.

He wandered far, and he wander'd long,
   Till he found in that western land,
A strange old man, who sadly gazed
   On something in his hand.

" Now what hast thou found, thou strange old man ?
   Now what has thou there ?" said he ;
He turned not his eye, as he made reply,
   " 'Tis nought but a gwidgy-gwee."

" And where didst thou find that curious thing ?
   I pray thee answer me."
" 'Twas down between the hepse and the durns
   I got that gwidgy-gwee.

The Professor could speak French, Latin, and Greek,
  Dutch, Hebrew, and Chinee,
But he knew not a hepse, and he knew not a durns,
  And he knew not a gwidgy-gwee.

And he could claim to know the name
  Of every curious creature ;
With a glance of the eye he'd classify
  Its every salient feature.

For he knew a dinotherium
  From its snout down to its tail ;
He'd construct a megalosaurus,
  Nor miss a fin nor scale.

He'd magnify a small microbe
  As big as a bumble bee ;
Tho' he knew them all, both great and small,
  He knew not a gwidgy-gwee.

So he drooped his eyes, and he bowed his head,
  And a sad, shamed man was he,
For he dared not acknowledge for the sake of his
  That he knew not a gwidgy-gwee. [College

" Pray show me that wondrous thing
  Which thou hast found ? " said he.
He turned his head, but the man had fled,
  The man with the gwidgy-gwee.

The Professor he took his staff in hand,
    And wandered forth to see
If he could find that curious thing,
    They call a gwidgy-gwee.

And whenever he saw a western hill—
    " Is this the ' hepse ' ? " asked he ;
And whenever a stream, " Is this the ' durns,'
    Where they find the gwidgy-gwee ? "

He sought where grew, in aspect lew,
    The skedgwith and the scow,
And he routed the sleepy hedgy-boar,
    And the lively padgypaow.

And on many a bank, where tall and rank,
    Midst twining dralyers free,
The lizamamoo and the keggas grew,
    Under the hagglan tree.

He sought, where cool in their reedy pool,
    Were yellow quilkins found,
And on the land, where the pillyers stand,
    And the muryans swarm around.

He sought where the sides of old Dinsûl
    Slope to the sunny south,
Where hollensmoks and fragrant tags,
    And britons, were in blowth.

And in many a huggo, dark and damp,
    Where oft the wild waves roar ;
And he raked the bullies and croggan shells
    From the pollons on the shore.

He sought, in the candle-teening time,
    When the dark rare-mice flew out,
And the dumbledories hummed their song,
    As they flew the fields about

He the local antiquarians joined,
    And they showed him after tea,
For British huts some old pigs' crows,
    But never a gwidgy-gwee.

Weary, and long, and vain was the quest,
    And a sad, bent man was he,
When one dark, cold day, he met by the bay
    The man of the gwidgy-gwee.

" Now stand thou still, thou strange old man,—
    Move not a step ! " said he,
" For, by my degree in zoology,
    Thou shalt not escape from me."

" For in peace or strife, in death or life,
    Thou shalt reveal to me,
What is that most mysterious thing
    That's named a gwidgy-gwee."

With a swift affrighted glance around
  The old man whispered then,
With mouth to ear, that word of fear—
  " 'Tis nought but a goozey-gen ! "

MORAL.

My youthful friend, to me attend,
  This precept keep in view ·
Don't be led astray by things that may
  To you seem strange and new.

Remember this fact   tho' fine names attract,
  They don't mean much, do you see ?
For there's many a common goozey-gen
  Disguised as a gwidgy-gwee.

———

The Battle of Cury Church Town.

" That battle was fought down there, exactly in front of old John
Chegwidden's blacksmith's shop door "—*Local Chronicler*

" 'Twas a month come Saturday that a stranger came this way,
And he sought within my cottage a shelter from the rain ,
As we sat before the grate he asked me to relate
The story of the battle 'twixt the Saxon and the Dane.

B

" 'Twas a thousand years or so, or it might be more, ago,
That the Danes against the Saxons were marching in their
         might ;
They were by Canute led, and each had hair so red
That any bull' d have coosed him had he shown within his
         sight.

" 'Twas in the harvest time, the kurning it was prime,
And the tummals were not bad, so I've heard my father
         say ;
They'd a lot of hurling weather when they got the corn
         together,
But the season had been catching when they saved their
         crop of hay

" Said the stranger : ' Do you know, it seems hardly *apropos*
To the story you're relating to talk of corn and hay.'
Said I : Father lived to be rather more than ninety-three,
And he always told the story in this interesting way.

" The Saxon army stood all erect, as soldiers should,
And King Arthur bravely led them, in a suit of armour
         bright,
And as he did espy the proud glance of each eye,
He knew that one and all of them were dagging for a fight.

" Just down by them two gates was a splat of rare potates,
Which were planted in a voyer ,—they were purty for to see,
Of a sort called ' early-fame '—you may have heard the
         name,—
And—here that stupid stranger went and interrupted me.

'Excuse me if I fancy there's a want of relevancy
In those last remarks you made ; you probably are right,
But I don't see that those gates and the voyer of potates
Have any close connection with that sanguinary fight.'

" Said I : Stranger, you may know all the story, and if so,
I will thank you to inform me just what it ought to be,
But I venture for to doubt if you know all about
The thing as did my father, who was over ninety-three.

" Bare-headed, and with speed, upon a gallant steed,
Came a dark and dusty horseman from down the Towan way ;
And he paused to let them know that the leader of the foe
Was forbidding of the water from coming in Mount's Bay.

"I wish you had been there to have seen that rider's mare ;
You never could have matched her for beauty, or for speed ;
She was, my father said, by Atty Harris bred,
And her dam she was a pony of the old Goonhilly breed.

" The Lawrences of Clahar had a colt from that same mare ;
The avage—here that stranger interrupted with a sneer—
' I am under the impression this is a fresh digression,
And you won't get to the fighting if I listen for a year.'

" Said I, as I arose,—sooner than you suppose
We shall get to the fighting, if you interfere with me ;
My father never would, have such interruption stood,
And he often told the story when over ninety-three,

" I put on my clean gook to-day,
    And went to fetch some barm,—
When I stanked 'pon a slaw-cripple,
    Down there by Hodge's farm.
I screeched, and with a furzey-more
    His back I tried to bang,
But aw twingled like an angle-dutch,
    And crawled into a drang."

*   *   *

FROM the well a maiden came,
    With her pitchers coarse and brown,
By the wicket's rustic frame,
    For awhile she laid them down ;
Lightly from her forehead flung
    Wavy locks of chestnut hair,
Which in sweet confusion clung
    Round her face, so fresh and fair.
Posed a form whose supple grace
    Far outvied the sculptor's art,
Which no cunning hand could trace,
    Or to rigid stone impart.
E'en the strangely rude design
    Of her coarse and meagre dress
Failed to hide one curve or line
    Of her matchless loveliness.
Sweetest she of all the choice
    Fresh wild flowers she stood among,
While with clear untutored voice
    She carolled forth a mirthful song.

SONG.

Oh, once I had a shiner,
   And a boshy man was he,
As prinky and as coxey
   As ever he could be,
But a maiden came one day
And fencaged his heart away.

Her face was full of murfles,
   She davered was and brown,
She wore a rory-tory hat,
   And a shally-go-naked gown,
And her fine fligs so gay
They slocked his heart away.

When next I have a shiner
   No more kybosh for me,
Some slawterpooch I'll marry
   Who'll ever constant be,
And not by maidens gay
Be lightly led away.

*   *   *

THEN, the narrow path ascending,
   Came a rustic, homeward wending ;
I looked at him benignly,
And I said in accents kindly :—
" Tho' thou art but a peasant,
   Thy life is bright and pleasant ,
Not the mighty, not the wealthy

Are so happy, are so healthy ;
So envy not the great,
With their splendour and their state ;
Thou hast no vain ambition
To better thy condition ;
To wear the golden fetters
That do enslave thy betters.
Man unsophisticated,
Tell me—art thou not sated
With the comfort of thy lot,
With the beauty of thy cot.
For the blessings of thy station
Dost thou feel appreciation?"
Tho' I spoke half jocosely,
He answered me morosely,
As he turned towards the door,
Only this and nothing more :—

" From early candleteening,
    I've been down in Clodgy Moor,
A-stanking o'er the tubbans,
    And just stagged in the voor ;
'Twas so clisty that the gruter
    Would hardly turn the coam ;
I've been rooging till I've hardly
    Sprall enough to take me home.

" I'm colder than a quilkin,
    I am leary, I am thurl,
I am aching all across the cheens,
    I have pains here in the whirl ;

F'rall now all of a croop
   I stuggy was and strong,
But I've louster'd till I'm hardly
   Able for to sloot along.

" I'd gurty-milk for breakfast,
   For crowst I'd not a crevan,
For dinner I'd a hoggan,
   Just as savoury as a leaven ;
And the only bit of lewth I had
   When it came to a skew
Was a high bunch of kekezza,
   That 'pon a gurgey grew.

" I don't like to be tatchy,
   But I do get in a por
When some great plum head bucca
   Comes talking, like you are
'Bout the splendour of my lot,
   As if 'twere fairly dazzling ;
Till I'm mazed enough to scat
   Thy great bussa-head a mazzling."

      *   *   *

Slowly I turned away, broken and sad,
Answering neither word, good nor bad ;
Here from my sorrows I'd hoped for release,
In this fancied abode of refinement and peace.

Thought in this Eden there ne'er could have been
Aught that was coarse, or sordid, or mean;
Now all my illusions have vanished away :
What I thought porcelain was coarse common clay.

The Luckless Poet.

" I SUPPOSE you heard about our Sampey.   He is a bit
of a poet, and no wonder,—for his mother's brother was
married to a cousin of Henry Quick, the Zennor poet; so
it do run a bit in the family.   Well, Sampey came home
t'other night lame as a cat.   Says I : ' Hallo, Sampey !
where hast a ben ?'   Says he, quite short like : ' Minding
my own business.'   Says I : ' Sampey, thee'st got the siatic.'
Says he : ' That's so much as you do knaw about it.'
Says I : ' I do knaw , I've had it scores of times.'   Says
he : ' If you've had it, I hope you liked it.'   And off he
went to bed.   Next day he was very bad—couldn't set,
stand, nor go.   In the evening he got pen, ink and paper,
and begun to write poetry, but he wouldn't show it to us.
But t'other day Peggy was brushing his cloase, and she
found the paper in his waistcoat pocket.   This is what he
wrote " :—

A   POEM.

I promised her I'd call laast night
    If nothing came to hender,
So I steered up towards the light
    In Uncle Sampey's winder.

The clock was striking eight as I
  The garden gate was hitchin';
I silently unlatched the door,
  And walked into the kitchen.

Thinks I, as I took off my hat,
  I'm glad I'm safely landed.
The house was looking fresh as paint,
  The floor was sweept and sanded.
The cheldren all had gone to bed,
  The old folks gone to mittin',
And Sarah Ann sat by the fire,
  A-busy with her knittin'.

The chimney-piece was trimmed around
  With bay, and box, and holly ·
I said " Good evenin', Sarah Ann ; "
  She said " Good evenin', Solly "
And as she turned her eyes on me,
  She looked so purty—bless her !
The fire-light shined around the room,
  And danced upon the dresser.

The old cat purred before the fire,
  A-blinking at its flashes ;
The teak'le was singing curls
  Among the turfy-ashes.
The dog got up and wagged his tail,
  My fingers gently lickin';
The old clock wagged the pendulum,
  And kept on with his tickin'.

I said, says I—and cleared my throat,
  And moved in her direction—
" Shall I set by your side, my dear ?"
  Said she—" I've no objection."
So, stooping down, I took her hand,
  Our fingers interlocking,—
And sat—upon the niddle which
  She'd used to mend her stockin' !

———

Ann of Market-jew.

(Not the original title to this little piece.)

A BALLAD.

COME, all you lads and lasses,
  A tale to you I'll tell,—
But first bring the burndockie,
  For I love that liquor well :—
Young Guy was Lord of Ludgvan,*
  A noble youth, and true,
He loved a gentle maiden,
  Sweet Ann of Market-jew.

---

* Ludgvan, or Ludgvan Lês, was one of the most ancient and important manors in West Cornwall.

Of many a goodly manor
   Was stout Sir Guy the Lord,
And many a sturdy vassal
   At his command drew sword ;
But from long years of conflict
   A deadly feud there grew,
Between the Lords of Ludgvan
   And Chiefs of Market-jew.

Out spoke her cruel uncle,
   And thus to her did say :—
" Oh ! youthful love is fleeting,
   As the storm-driven spray,
And, like a fire of griglans,
   'Tis fierce, but very brief :
Thou ne'er shalt wed our foeman,
   So put away thy grief."

Now weaker than a purvan,
   She felt when this she heard,
And colder than a conker-bell,
   Her heart turned at that word ;
Whisht as a dying winnard
   She looked, but nought did say :—
Young Guy he fondly kissed her,
   Then proudly turned away.

Now he has taken his armour,
   Which hung within his hall,
And he has taken the stoutest steed
   That champed within his stall ;

The stools, the books, tin-tacks, and cheers
My wife has carr'd them all up steers.
She've burnt up all the shavings too
For fear that they would get wet through.
Ef she continues in this plight
Of agitation, fear and fright,
She'll scat up every crock and kittle
For fear the say will rust the mittle.
And yet sometimes I think, my dear,
We needn't give away to fear,
The wave mayn't be as people say
(I saw a rainbow t'other day);
But ef the wave should on us burst,
I think, my dear, we knaw the worst;
We knaw that Noah's ark arn't nigh,
But Peter's boat * is handy by.
Though Ararat is far away,
We may land somewhere near the bay.
Some of the hills around are high—
We may drift as fur's Carn Kie;
And ef the wind don't blaw agen us
We may fitch up to Castle-an-Dinas; †
Ef we should chance to drift so near
We're sure to come and see ee, dear;

---

* Peter's boat—a small ferry-boat.   Peter was one of the Mount
boatmen.

† Castle-an-Dinas—a hill in the parish of St Columb.

And as we all may be wet through,
And tired, and cold, and hungry too,
Tell Mrs Baker, we desire
The kittle may be on the fire,
For we shall want a cup of tay
After such a voyage, and say
A heavy cake will do to eat ;
Or, if she likes, a joint of meat.
This will with Mary's letter go.
With love, your own dear brother,

JOE.

Nan of Castle Gate.

A BALLAD WITH A MORAL

Now, ladies, listen unto me,
   While I to you relate
The strange, but truthful history,
   Of Nan, of Castle Gate.

This maiden for her beauty rare
   Was far and wide renowned,
The fairest and the proudest lass
   In all the country 'round.

Her father was a cottager,
　Who laboured in a mine ;
His dearest wish—that his fair maid
　Might be a lady fine.

Her mother, who ambitious was,
　From morn to eve did toil,
In order that her dainty child
　Should not her fingers soil.

Now how to work embroidery,
　Or crochet, she did know ;
She could a slipper work in wool
　With roses on the toe.

But she could neither milk the cow,
　Nor cook the family meals ;
She could not wash, nor make a shirt,
　Nor darn her stocking heels.

For she had done but little else
　Since she came in her teens,
But sat and read romantic tales,
　In penny magazines.

She pondered o'er such silly tales,
　As in such books you see,
Of haughty nobles who had wed
　With maids of low degree.

Now many rustic lovers came,
    And woo'd, but woo'd in vain,
For every honest son of toil
    She treated with disdain.

" The one," this scornful damsel said,
    " Who'd win me for his bride,
Must boast of high and noble birth,
    And in his carriage ride."

She dressed her in her Sunday's best,
    She brushed her flaxen curls,
And watched the road from day to day,
    For passing dukes and earls.

She waited weeks, she waited months ;
    Alas ! it was her fate
To find the dukes, and earls, were few
    That passed by Castle Gate.

When years had passed, this haughty maid
    Less highly did aspire—
She would have wed a baronet,
    Or even an esquire.

Time passed ; there came a gentle youth
    Who won the maid in marriage ;
Tho' not of noble birth, it might
    Be said he keeps his carriage.

For proudly now they drive about,
  Through all the western land,
Selling, from out a donkey cart,
  New brooms and scouring-sand.

MORAL.

Now, mothers, who have daughters fair,
  Don't bring them up too grand,
Or you may find they're hardly fit
  For selling scouring-sand.

———

Nanny Guy.

A BALLAD.

" Why sitting here alone, fair maid?
    The eve grows cold and dim;
  Long since the noisy rooks have sought
    The elms of Old Bochym.
  This is no fitting place for thee,
    On Carrac-hir's rough stone,
  Then tell me why, fair Nanny Guy,
    Thou'rt sitting here alone."

" In haste, from Garrah's burning towers,
 I have in terror fled,
For, struck by cruel Grockal's hand,
 My father there lies dead.
Of all that band of trusty men,
 Who served Sir Hugh De Guy,
Some are dead, and some have fled,
 And some in dungeon lie."

" ' Fair Maid,' young Robin Kelvie said,
 ' Thou nothing hast to fear ;
My gallant steed is standing by,
 My merry men are near ;
And to my Hall, in Lampra Vale,
 Thou home shalt go with me,
Where thou shalt be my mother's care,
 And none shall dare harm thee.' "

" Now welcome home, my own brave son,
 With all thy gallant band ;
But who is this, so fair and sad,
 Thou leadest by the hand ? "
" Oh ! this is murdered Garrah's child,
 That I've brought home to thee,
And she shall be thy daughter dear,
 Her mother, thou shalt be."

" Now take thy steed, my faithful page,
 Ride fast, and do not spare,
And rouse the lads of High-far-off,
 The gallant youths of Clahar ;

Likewise all Meaver Wartha's Men,
　　To arm them for the fray ;
And meet me all, by Herlan Pool,
　　An hour before the day."

" Why crept ye down the stair, my son,
　　As if I might not hear ?
Why armed are all thy trusty men
　　With sword, and axe, and spear ? "
" We go to hunt e'er break of day
　　Among the banks of Clahar,
To rouse the wild wolf from his den,
　　The fierce boar from his lair. "

" No whimpering hound doth wake, my son,
　　The silence of the night ;
And thou, instead of coat of green,
　　Art clad in armour bright."
" My hounds will follow soon mother,
　　Thou hast no cause for fear ;
I wear my arms in youthful sport,—
　　Farewell, my mother dear."

" What hast thou home from hunting brought ?
　　No dead game do I see,
But bloody swords, and wounded men
　　Thou bringest home to me ;
Thou sittest heavy on thy steed,
　　And thou art wounded sore,
Oh ! was it fang of cruel wolf ?
　　Or tusk of angry boar ? "

" We sought not bear, nor wolf, mother,
    Among the banks of Clahar ;
  But we sought Grockal's cruel lord,
    And smote him in his lair ;
  We stormed his gates, and scaled his walls ;
    It was a bloody fray ,
  We slew his men, and burnt his den—
    An hour before the day."

" There was joy in lone Praze Marrack,
    In Meaver and Penhale ;
  And there was merry feast and sport
    All down the Lampra Vale ;
  On Carrac-hir, and Garrah-rocks,
    The festive fires blazed high,
  When Robin Kelvie won the hand
    Of gentle Nanny Guy.

A Wicked Alligator.

In a spirit of true aetological scepticism the *Granta* furnishes the following ingenious explanation of the remarkable story in which a Cornish woman and a Lizard were implicated.—" The origin of the legend is clear. This lady had for years, doubtless, lived *at* the Lizard. Then it became that she lived *on* a Lizard. Then that a Lizard lived *on* her—next *in* her. Hence the wonderful account which has so thrilled us this week."—*Globe*, February, 1892.

Come, all you gentle readers,
　I pray you not to laugh
When you see this narration
　In the " *Cornish Telegraph* ; "
For 'tis not my intention
　For idle mirth to cater
When I tell to you the story
　Of the wicked Alligator.

Across the breezy Morraps
　That faced St. Michael's Bay
A woman gently wandered,
　And pleasant was the day ;

She drank out of a brooklet
  (Or so says the narrator),
And swallowed with the water
  An embryo Alligator.

But seeming not contented
  With very careful housing,
The creature soon awakened,
  And commenced some nice carousing ;
And the woman seemed possessed
  Of an active nutmeg-grater,
So was she scratched and scoured
  By that wicked Alligator.

For in the small apartment,
  Where he'd obtained possession,
He played at earthquakes, football,
  And Sunday school procession ,
Not even Jonah to the whale
  Was such an agitator—
As to that gentle woman
  Was that wicked Alligator.

She rushed off to the doctor,
  Who was a man of might ·
" Oh ! doctor, dearest doctor,
  Can you set my 'innards' right
I've such commotion in the
  Region of my equator,
And I know that I'm the victim
  Of an awful Alligator."

The doctor looked profound,
   And upward turned his eyes,
And then he felt her pulse,
   And viewed her tongue likewise ;
He turned him to his books,
   And searched each commentator
To find a sure prescription
   For an active Alligator.

From many a pot and bottle,
   He took powders, drops, and paste,
And put them in a mortar,
   And mixed them up in haste ;
And thus, with potent drugs, he
   Prepared a circulator—
That would move, like a tornado,
   That wretched Alligator.

Now, Beecham's pills are active,
   And Cockle's pills are strong ;
And Mother Seigel's syrup
   Can make things move along ;
But these are balm compared with
   The potent detonator,
The doctor there prepared, for
   That wretched Alligator.

Ah ! little does the lambkin,
   So full of playful life,
Reck of the dreadful shambles,
   And cruel butcher's knife ;

And little did that creature,
  Of commotion—the creator—
Think human foes were plotting
  Against an Alligator

One gulp ! the pill was swallowed !
  And soon there did begin,
A strife as if that woman,
  A volcano had within ;
But soon her troubled throat
  Became an active crater,
And quickly it ejected
  That wicked Alligator.

The creature hopped about ;
  The woman fetched a howl ,
But soon she "scat the life
  Out of en, with a showl "
Then took the padgypaow
  Unto a wise curator,
Who, with spirits in a bottle,
  Put that wicked Alligator

If credence to this story
  You venture to refuse,
You'll be severely censured
  By the " *Western Morning News* ; "
For is it not attested
  By the local Registrator,
Who has seen both the woman
  And the bottled Alligator.

MORAL.

Now, all you padgypaows,
    So frisky and so gay,
Be careful as you gambol
    Around St. Michael's Bay ;
Or you may chance to meet with
    That awful devastator—
A pill, made by the doctor,
    That slew the Alligator.

The Song of the Brush.

DRESSED with scrupulous care,
    And scented like a rose,
A youth, he stood, with his foot on a chair,
    A-brushing of his clothes.
'Twas on his wedding morn ;
    And with voice as clear as a thrush,
In a firm and decided tone,
    He sang " The song of the brush."

Brush, brush, brush,
    Though time is flying fast ;
Brush, brush, brush,
    Though 'tis eleven o'clock and past.

No matter where I'm going,
    No matter in what I'm dressed,
'Tis brush, brush, brush,
    Trousers, and coat, and vest

Brush, brush, brush,
    Though the carriage is at the gate,
Brush, brush, brush,
    Though the priest at the altar doth wait;
Though bride and bridesmaids, and all,
    Are fretting at delay,
If I can't brush in time.
    I'll be married some other day.

You know I can't endure
    Wet, nor dust, nor dirt,
I'll not have a speck upon my clothes,
    Nor a stain upon my shirt
I won't go dirty to church,
    But brush myself first—and then,
For fear a speck of dust remains,
    I'll brush myself over again.

His gloves were on his hands,
    His hat was on his head,
His friends all told him 'twas getting late,
    But in spite of all they said,
He kept his foot on the chair.
    And, with voice as clear as a thrush,
In a firm and decided tone,
    He sang the song of the brush.

D

Still drifting on its errant way,
   It nears the rugged Northern land ;
Past jutting cape, and dented bay,
The currents toss'd it in their play,
   Till where—on old Cornubia's strand,
The wild waves break with sullen roar
   In their incessant ebb and flow—
This Southern waif was cast ashore
   On the white beach of Sandy Vro.*

Soon found, and stripped with eager speed
From clinging worm, and tangled weed—
   By those who, awe-struck at the sight
Of the prone god, did solemnly
   Convey it up the dizzy height,
Unto a little town hard by.
   There, 'gainst a Christian temple's wall—
Erected by a pious hand,
   Just where the noontide sun-beams fall,
The heathen god was placed to stand,
   An idol in a Christian land.

---

* A small inlet in the Mullion cliffs, opposite the Gull Rock.

I Think of Thee.

A PEACEFUL scene   a love-sick youth
   Against a grassy bank was leaning ;
Around was many a forest glade,
   With leafy coppice intervening ;
A brooklet murmured at his feet.
   The woods with songs of birds were ringing ;
Sweeter, and far above them all,
   He thought he heard his loved one singing :—

SONG.

The weary sun has sunk to rest,
   The butterfly has left the flowers,
The blythe skylark has sought its nest,
   The wood-doves coo in leafy bowers—
I sit beneath a forest tree
   And think of thee.

The evening star proclaims the night,
   The busy streamlet murmuring flows,
Its wavelets dance in pale moonlight,
   And the dewdrops deck the fragrant rose—
I sit beneath a forest tree
   And think of thee.

CHARMS

Charms once used by the ancient fortune-telling dames, or "witch-doctors," of the surrounding districts, and given to the Author by their descendants. Several others, once in his possession, have, by accident, been destroyed.

Charm for turning Cream to Butter.

" Come, butter, come ,
Come, butter, come ,
Peter's waiting at the gate,
Waiting for a buttered cake ,
Come, butter, come."

Charm for Toothache.

" As Peter sat weeping upon a marble stone, our Saviour passed by, and said · Peter why weepest thou ?' Peter said unto Him 'I have got the toothache' And our Saviour said · ' Arise, and be sound , and whosoever keeps this in memory, or in writing, will never have the tooth-ache.' "

Charm for Burns.

" Three wise men came from the East,
    One carried fire, two carried frost ;
    Out fire, and in frost,
    In the name of the Father, Son, and Holy Ghost."

Charm for a Kennel on the Eye.

" Simon and Gaus went to our Lord Jesus Christ, and asked Him what to do against pins, pearls, and webs. Our Lord and Saviour, Jesus Christ, answered and said : ' Simon and Gaus, from your eyes let red fall, from your eyes let black fall. Eyes be eyes ! Eyes be eyes ! Eyes be eyes ! In the name of the Father, and of the Son, and of the Holy Ghost. Amen. Amen. Amen.' "

Charm for Stopping Bleeding.

" As Christ was born in Bethlehem, and baptized in the river Jordan, He said to the water ' Be still.' So shall thy blood. By the blessing of God the Father, God the Son, and God the Holy Ghost Pray God it may be so. I hope it will be so Amen Amen."

Charm that may be employed in any case without doing harm.

" Holy kai, holy kie,
    Tommy's nose will be better by-and-bye.
    Up, sun—down, moon ;
    Tommy's nose will be better soon

LOCAL

PROVERBS AND PHRASES.

———————

" A change of work is as good as touchpipe."

" A clout is better than a hole out."

" A slut never wants a clout while her apron lasts out."

" All abroad, like Mary Miles."

" All of a whiddle, like a dead lamb's tail."

" All one side, like a crab going to gaol "

" All on one side, like Smoothy's wedding."

" All behind, like a cow's tail "

" Always head and chief, like Jimmy Eellis 'mong the cats."

" Always on the ran-dan, like cousin Ann Harry's gander."

" A nuisance to a field of tinkers."

" As thick as inklemakers."

" Boys to bed, dogs to doors, and maidens to clean up the
ashes "

" Cold as a quilkin."

" Either staring or stark mad."

" Gaping like a duck against thunder."

" Going like a dog tailpiped."

" Good riddance to bad rummage."

" Grizzling like a badger."

" Gruffled up like an arish pig."

" Laughing like a piskey."

" Like a three ha'penny chick in a wheaten arish."

" Like An' Dinah Grey's old mare—when I'm up, I'm like
a flap, and when I'm down, can't rise."

" Like a cat in a bonfire, don't know which way to turn."

" Like Ludlow's dog—leaning against the wall to bark."

" Like Morvah downs—ploughed, not harrowed.

" Like the Mayor of Falmouth, who thanked God when the town gaol was enlarged."

" Like Ruan Vean men—don't knaw and weant be told "

" Like a pig with one ear "

" Mazed as a curley "

" More haste, more let."

" Neither ashore nor afloat."

" Poor as a coot."

" Proud in his own conceit, like Sammy Lidgey's chick."

" Staring like a stuck pig "

" Staving along like a man going to wreck."

" Scat to rags "

" Screech like a whitneck."

"Scrumped up like a hedgehog.

" Sick as a shag."

" Standing in his own light, like the Mayor of Market-jew."

" Stank on an angle-dutch and it will twine."

" Talking the fore leg of a horse off "

" The older you are the simpler you are, like the Fabies."

" They who can't schemey must louster."

" Wisht as a winnard."

" Worse than dirty butter and bally-ack."

RHYMES USED BY CHILDREN
IN PLAYING GAMES

" Hewery, hiery, hackery, heaven ,
    Hack a bone, crack a bone, ten or eleven.
    Baked, stewed, fried in the sun,
    Twiddlelem, twiddlelem, twenty-one."

———-

" Ena, mena, mora mi,
    Pisca lara, bora bi ,
    Eggs, butter, cheese, bread ,
    Stick, stack, stone, dead
    O, U, T, spells ' out.' "

———

" Hiery, diery, lumber lock,
    One a-mexey, two o'clock ,
    I sat, sing in the morning spring,
    Yellow, blue, black, green,
    In nine ; ' out.' "

GLOSSARY

OF THE

CORNISH DIALECT.

A

Abear. Abide, to bear, to endure. " I can't abear en."— Used negatively.

Abew, Abue. Above, up above.

Abroad. Asunder, open, in pieces. " You have left the door abroad." " Scat all abroad."

Actions. Pretence, affectation. " Lot of actions with em."

Addlegutter. A dirty, offensive pool or drain ; a cesspool.

Afeard. Afraid.

Afterwinding. The light Corn deposited between the heavy grain and the chaff.

E

Agate. Expectant. " All agate."

Agg. To push on, to incite, to egg.

Aglan, Aglet. The fruit of the hawthorn ; the hawthorn
    tree " Under the aglan tree."

Airy-mouse, Rare-mouse. The bat.

Aker, Aiker. " In his aiker," *i e.* in a congenial occupa-
    tion, doing something in which one takes an interest.

Alan. A hard, bare patch of ground.

Alantide. All Saints' Day.

Alley. A large marble, a taw.

Allish. Pale, sickly in appearance.

All-on-a-nupshot. Unexpectedly, in a great hurry.

Almond-nuts. Almonds.

Ampassy. Et cetra.

Anan ? What do you say ?

Angle-dutch. The earthworm.

Anist, Nist. Near, close to. " Don't come anist me."

Anointed. Mischievous, fond of fun. " An anointed lem.",

Apernt. An apron.

Apple-bird. The chaffinch.

Apple-bee, Apple-drane. The wasp.

Aps. The aspen tree

Arish. Stubble. " Barley arish "

Arg. To argue

Arm-wrist. The wrist.

Arrant. An errand, a message.

Arrere Wonderful, strange

Arry. Any.

Ascrode. Astride.

Asew, Sew. Dry. " The cow is asew "

Assneger. The ass.

Attle. Rubbish, refuse (A mining term)

Auvsis, Auvice. The eaves of a house.

Avage. Stock or breed " The avage is good."

Avore. Before

Aw. He, it.

Ax. Ask. " Did e axe en ? "

B

Backlong, Backalong. Formerly , the road just traversed.

Backsyfore. Forth and back, the reverse way.

Bagaroot. A Swede turnip (rootabaga)

Baggle. To muffle, to swathe.

Bal. To shout, to bawl " Balling and 'oll'ing."

Bal. A mine

Balk. To place in layers or rows (A term used in pilchard curing)

Ballyrag. To bully, to revile, to abuse.

Balm. A false imputation , a story told in jest.

Bal-maidens. Girls employed on surface work on mines.

Balsh. Stout cord.

Balshag. Coarse woollen cloth.

Bamfer. To worry, to harass, to torment.

Banger. A whopper.

Bank-up. To heap up, as clouds gather before rain.

Bannel. The broom.

Bare-ridged. To ride bare-backed, or without a saddle.

Bare-vamped. To stand in one's stockings; without shoes.

Bar-ire. A crow bar.

Barragan. Fustian.

Barristers. Bannisters.

Barning. Phosphorescent. "The sea is barning."

Bassam. Wild broom; a complication of colours occasioned by a bruise.

Beal. The bill (of a bird, etc.)

Bealing. Hatching. "The eggs are bealing."

Bean. A hazel rod for binding wood into faggots.

Bearn. A child.

Beat. To cut off turf from land; turf cut for fuel.

Beat-burrow. A heap of weeds or turf partly burnt, or collected for burning.

Beat-burning. The burning of turf heaps in fields for manure.

Bed-ale. Ale brewed for a christening.

Bedoled. Dismal, low-spirited, dull, heavy with trouble.

Bed-tye. A feather bed.

Bee-butt. A bee-hive.

Beety. To mend fish nets.

Bell-metal. The brass pan in which preserves are made.

Belong. To be accustomed; to be due. "He belongs to go every day." The 'bus belongs to start soon."

Belve. To bellow.

Bender. Something exceedingly large.

Berryin. A funeral.

Besting. Deciding. " Besting whether to go or no."

Betterfit. To greater advantage; wiser; better. " Better-fit you'd held your tongue."

Bettermost. Best; advantage gained. " Her bettermost bonnet." " I got the bettermost of them."

Bettix, Biddix. Beat-axe; a mattock.

Bever. To shiver with cold.

Bevering. Shaking, or shivering with cold.

Bib. A blind. (A kind of small fish.)

Bibble. To tipple.

Biggan. A nightcap without a border.

Bilders. The plant *heracleum sphondylium*, or cow parsnip. In the North of Cornwall the *œnanthe crocata* is called " Bilder."—This plant is very poisonous.

Bisgan. A shield made like the finger of a glove, and used for a sore finger.

Biskey. A biscuit.

Bittle, Beetle. A mattock; a thatcher's mallet for driving spars.

Bitter-weed. A disgraceful person. " She's a bitter weed.'

Black-head. A kind of boil.

Black-worm. The cockroach.

Blanketing-shirts. A sort of smock-frock made of heavy woollen.

Blast. A cold; sudden inflammation.

Blinch. To sight, to catch a glimpse.

Blind-bucca-davy. Blind man's buff.

Blink. A spark.

Blog, Bloggy. Thick set, stout. " A bloggy little horse."

Blood-sucker. The sea anemone.

Bloody-warrior. The dark wallflower.

Blowth. Blossom ; in flower. " The May is in blowth."

Bobbin-joan. Round excrescences on potatoes.

Bobble. A pebble.

Bobble. A ground swell.

Boft. Bought. " Boften bread."

Boggle. To be checked by a difficulty, as a horse unable to move its load.

Boggle. To lie.

Boiling. Crowd, family, lot. " The whole boiling."

Bol. An iron ladle used for dipping water.

Bolt. A drain.

Booba. A sort of torch made of rags and dipped in train oil ; a wick.

Boots-and-shoes. The columbine.

Bosh. Display.

Boshy. Foppish, smart, conceited

Bougan. The large end of a piece of wood or timber.

Boyer. A rock-drill.

Boy's-love. Southernwood.

Braggaty. Spotted, mottled.

Bran Quite " Bran new."

Brandiz, Brandys. An iron tripod for supporting a kettle, etc., over the fire

Brandiz-ways. Triangular.

Brave. Hearty, well, in good health. "How are ee?"—
"Brave, thank ee."

Brave-few. A good many, a fair quantity.

Brave-flink. To be almost able to do a thing; to nearly
accomplish "Aw didn't do en fitty, but aw gave en
a brave flink"

Breachy. A term applied to cattle given to climbing
fences.

Bread-and-dippy. Barley bread and thin cream

Breek, Brik. A small tear or rent in a garment.
"There's not a breek in it"

Brembles. Brambles

Brink. A fish's gill.

Brit. A tiny fish, smaller than a sprat

Briton. The thrift or sea-pink. (St. Michael's Mount)

Broach. A long stick used in fastening ropes in thatch.

Brose (of heat). A fierce heat.

Brouse. A thicket, also short furze, ferns, etc

Brush. A nosegay.

Bruss. The dust and prickles from dried furze

Bucca. A scarecrow; a fool.

Buck, Buckaboo. A ghost; a hobgoblin

Buck. A term applied to milk when it is affected by
heat or some other cause, and is rendered unfit for
use. "The buck is in the milk."

Buckhorn. Dried salt whiting

Buckle-up. To shrink, to draw together.

Budpicker. The bullfinch.

Buddy. A clump, a thick bunch, a cluster "A regular
buddy."

Buffle-head. A simpleton.

Bulch. To push with a horn, to butt.

Bullgrannick. A snail.

Bulljig, Bullhorn. A snail.

Bully. A pebble.

Burndockie. A liquor made of hot cider, sugar and eggs.

Burn. A bundle of hay, straw, furze, etc., tied by a rope called the " burn-rope."

Bus. An unweaned calf.

Bushed. Confirmed.

Bussa. A coarse earthen pot ; a fool ; a simpleton.

Bustious. Full ; corpulent.

Butt. A bee-hive ; an ox-cart.

Butter-and-eggs. The double daffodil.

Butts. A disease in horses.

Busy. Requires. " Busy all your strength to lift it." " Busy all your time."

C

Cab. Mess ; disorder.

Cabby. Dirty, sticky, untidy.

Cabbed, Cabbed-over. Handled, messed about.

Cader. A frame on which fishing lines are kept.

Cadge. To beg.

Cadging. Begging, asking charity.

Cage. A set; often applied to teeth. " A cage of teeth."

Cage-of-bones. A skeleton.

Caggled, Cagged. Caked, ingrained.

Camel. The camomile plant.

Candleteening. Twilight.

Capparouse, Caperhouse. A row, an uproar, a hubbub.

Care. The mountain ash.

Catch-up. To dry quickly; to work with speed, etc. " To catch-up my churs."

Catching. Unsettled, changeable.

Cat-in-the-pan. A somersault.

Caudle. To slop, to mess; to get into a difficulty; also a difficulty; a slop, etc.

Caudly. Dirty, murky. " Caudly weather."

Caudler. An untidy, slovenly worker.

Caunch. A mess, confusion.

Caunting. Diagonal, athwart.

Caunted. Athwart, tilted.

Cawnse, Caunse. A causeway, a paved road.

Cazier, Cayer. A kind of hand sieve for sifting grain.

Ceague. A cheat, a deceiver, a rogue.

Censure. To estimate; to think; to reckon.

Chacks. The cheeks.

Chack. To parch, to dry. " I'm chackin thirst."

Chacky-cheese. The seeds of the mallow.

Chad. A young bream.

Chall. A cattle house

Cheat. A false shirt front.

Cheeld Chiel. A child.

Cheeld-vean. A term of endearment, meaning "little child."

Cheens. The loins; the quarters of a house.

Cheese. Pounded apples ready for pressing.

Cheening. The sprouting of grain, etc.

Cherks. Cinders.

Chets. Kittens.

Chibble. A kind of small onion.

Chickell. The wheat-ear.

Chiff-chaff. The chaff-finch.

Chiffer. To drive a bargain, to haggle.

Chill. An iron lamp for burning train oil.

Chimbly. A chimney.

Chillbladder. Chilblain.

Ching. The chin.

Chip. The foot of a plough.

Chiterlings. Small entrails

Chuff. Healthy-looking, full-faced.

Chuck. The throat. "Dry about the chuck."

Chuck. To choke. "He's chucked."

Chuck-cheelds. The chad

Chuckle-head. A fool.

Chur. A small job; household duties. "Catch-up your churs"

Churing. Charing.

Churer. A charwoman.

Clam. A footbridge.

Clammered. Ailing, weak, sickly.

Claps. A clasp.

Clean-off. Cleverly; completely

Clever. Tolerably well , in good health.

Clibby, Clisty. Sticky, adhesive

Clich. To fasten, to latch " Clich the gate."

Click-handed, Click-pawed. Left-handed.

Clidgy. Sweets made of boiled sugar, and sold in sticks.

Cliders. Goose-grass.

Clink. A "lock-up," a gaol.

Clip, Click. A sudden sharp blow ; a box on the ear.

Cloam, Clome. Earthenware

Clodgy. Boggy, muddy. " Clodgy lane."

Clomen. Made of earthenware " Grinning like a clomen cat."

Clop. To limp.

Clopper. A lame person.

Clopping. Limping.

Clout. An old cloth or rag. " A dish clout "

Coajer's-wax. Shoemaker's-wax or pitch.

Cob. A crest of hair or feathers , the forelock.

Cob. A mixture of clay and straw for building purposes. " Cob walls."

Cobbing. Breaking ore into small pieces.

Cobbing-hammer. The hammer used in breaking ore.

Cobble-de-cut-nuts. Hazel-nuts.

Cob-nuts. Hazel-nuts , a game played with nuts strung on strings

Cock-hedge. A quickset hedge

Cockle-buttons. The burrs of the burdock.

Codge. An untidy, slovenly piece of work.

Codger. A slovenly worker.

Coffins. Depressions of the earth, caused by the under-mining of the ground.

Collybrand. Sheet lightning ; smut in corn, black ears of corn.

Come-by-chance. Accidental.

Comfortable. Easy-going, agreeable.

Compartner. A consort.

Condiddle. To swindle, to rob.

Conduddle. Conceit.

Conkerbell. An icicle.

Conuram. A name by which the early Methodists were regularly known throughout West Cornwall. (In common use from 80 to 100 years ago.)

Come-out. Quarrel, disturbance. "A purty come-out down there."

Cool. A trough in which salt pork, etc., is kept.

Cooram. Order, decorum. "Keep cooram."

Coose. To chase, to hunt, to pursue.

Coose. "In coose." Ready, prepared. "Get in coose avore they come."

Coose. "A coose of water." A "turn" of water.

Cooting. A thrashing.

Cooze. To gossip, to idle away time in talking.

Coozing. Gossiping.

Copper-finch. The chaff-finch.

Core. A "spell" of work. "He's on night core."

Corisy. Hatred, ill-feeling, ill-will.

Corncrake. The landrail.

Corniwillen. The lapwing.

Country. Ground, land, the natural strata of the earth. "Built against the country," *i.e.* built against hilly ground.

Cover-slut. One who takes the blame due to another; anything used to cover up dirt.

Cowle. A fish-basket.

Coxy. Pert, saucy.

Crabbed. Quirkish, artful.

Cracked. Insane.

Crafe. To mend hastily or loosely.

Craffing. Sewing, or mending clumsily.

Crake. A harsh cry.

Cravel. The lintel over a chimney.

Creem. To squeeze.

Creen. To grieve, to complain, to pine.

Creener. An ailing, sickly person.

Creening. Ailing, complaining. "A creening woman will live for ever."

Crevan. A dry, hard crust.

Creeved. Partly cooked; partly dry.

Crib. A slight luncheon.

Cribber. A small eater, a "picker."

Cricks. Dry sticks, hedgewood.

Cricket. A low stool.

Cricking. Collecting small articles of household use against marriage; gathering odds and ends; picking sticks.

Crickmole. A somersault.

Crim. To shiver with cold.

Cripple. A lame person.

Cripse. Crisp.

Cripse. To slightly crack or craze glass or earthenware.

Criss-cross-row. The alphabet. (So called because in the old horn books it was always headed with a cross.)

Crock. A three legged iron pot used for cooking purposes.

Crofts. Downs.

Croggan. A limpet shell.

Croom. A small quantity, a tiny bit   (Probably corruption of " crumb ")

Crow. A sty. " Pig's crow."

Crouging. Shuffling, walking heavily.

Croust. Lunch taken between meals.

Crowd. A fiddle , to purr.

Crowder. A fiddler.

Crowder. A "slow-coach," a dawdler.

Crowdy. To fiddle.

Crowding. Purring   " The cat's crowding."

Crowner. A coroner.

Crowning. An inquest.

Crop-of-the-bunch. The best, or prettiest of the lot or family.

Crow-sheaf. The sheaf that completes the gable of a mow of corn.

Cruddly. Curly

Cruds. Curds.

Cruel. Very, extremely " Cruel hard."

Crumbed. Bent or drawn together with cold.

Crumptins. Small deformed apples.

Cuckoo. The hare-bell or blue-bell

Cud. A quid of tobacco

Cuddling. Doing light work or jobs; working feebly. " Just able to cuddle along "

Cue. An iron protection on the heel of a boot or shoe; an ox shoe.

Cundard. A conduit.

Cuney, Cuny. Moss, lichen, mildew.

Curls. Carols

Custice. A blow across the hand with a rod.

Cussal, Cuzzle. Deceitful.

D

Daffer. A large quantity " A brave daffer."

Dafter, Douter. Daughter

Dag. A small hatchet

Dagging. Anxious, longing to do something " Dagging for a fight " " Dagging to know."

Daggings. Heavily laden, a large quantity " Daggings of them."

Dane. " Red-headed Dane." A term of contempt.

Daps. Likeness, counterpart.

Dash. An unbound faggot of furze.

Dash-an-darras. The stirrup-glass.

Dashy. Showy

Datch. To thatch.

Datcher. A thatcher.

Daugh, Daw. Dough.

Daver. To fade, to pine.

Davered. Faded, worn out.

Dead-and-alive. Without energy; dull; indifferent; lukewarm.

Deads. Subsoil; refuse.

Deal-seed. The fir-cone.

Deef. Deaf. "Deef as an adder."

Deef. Rotten; empty. "A deef apple."

Dewsnail. The slug.

Dicky. An over-jacket worn by working men.

Diddle. "Every little diddle." Tittle-tattle; every little ridiculous tale.

Didgan. A very small bit, a tiny piece.

Didgy. Small, tiny.

Dido. "A purty dido." A row, a great fuss.

Dig. A blow, a thrust. "A dig in the back."

Dig. To scratch.

Dilly. A light waggon.

Dilly-dallying. Trifling, hesitating, shilly-shallying.

Ding. To repeat over and over, to reiterate. "Ding, ding, ding, all the day long."

Dinged. Reiterated.

Dinsûl. St. Michael's Mount.

Dish. The dues paid to the lord of the mine.

Dishwasher, Dishwater. The water-wagtail

Dīsle, Dīzle. The thistle "Milky dīsle"

Dob, Dab. To throw.

Dob. A lump. "A great dob of earth."

Dobbett. Short, thick-set. "A regular dobbet."

Dock. The crupper of a saddle.

Doldrums. "In the doldrums." Low-spirited, cast down.

Dole. An ungainly bundle. "A great dole."

Doles. Small heaps of ore of equal size for weighing

Dorymouse. The dormouse.

Douter. *See* Dafter.

Down. Low-spirited, downcast. "Down in the mouth."

Downdanted. Disheartened, discouraged

Downses. Moors, downs. "Pradnack downses."

Downsouse. Outright, without beating about the bush,
to the point

Dowsing-rod. A forked twig of hazel or white thorn,
which, when carried over a lode or mineral vein, is
said to turn in the hand toward the ground.

Doxy. Smart, pretty "A doxy little bonnet."

Dralyers. Trailing plants or weeds, more especially the
wild convolvulus.

Dram. A swathe of corn.

Drang. An open drain or gutter, an open groove or
channel.

Drane, Apple-drane. The wasp

Drash. To thrash corn.

Drashel. A flail.

F

Draw. A kind of sledge.

Dredge-corn. A mixed crop of corn.

Dredgy-ore. Ore and stone mixed.

Dressel, Drexel. The threshold.

Dribs. Small sums of money, small debts, a small quantity. " Mary Anna collects the dribs."

Driggle. To dribble, to fall in drops, to ooze out slowly, to run feebly along. " Water driggling down."

Drilger. A great noise.

Drill-drolls. Trailing plants ; the wild convolvulus.

Dripshams. Last drops of liquid.

Drive. To drift.

Drivers. Fishing boats using drift-nets.

Driving-nets. Drift-nets carried by the " drivers."

Droke. A groove, a slight channel ; a slight hollow of the body.

Droll. A tale, an idle tale, legend.

Droolgey. Drulgy. Slow, heavy in movement.

Drop-curls. Long curls, ringlets.

Drow. To dry.

Drug. The drag (of a wheel).

Drule. To drivel.

Dry. The house in which the miners change their clothes.

Dryth. Dry weather or drought. " A scat of dryth."

Dubbet, Dobbet. Short, stumpy.

Duff. Suet pudding.

Duff. A blow ; a blow on a cow's udder with a calf's nose.

Dug-in-the-back. A game of " tig," the players stand- ing in a ring.

Dull. Hard of hearing, deaf.

Dumbledory, Dumbledrane. The cockchaffer.

Dunyon. A dungeon " Down in the dunyon."

Durk. Dark.

Durns. The frame of a door.

Dust. The chaff of corn.

Duzz. To buzz

E

Earth-ridge. Earth, round the sides of a field carted out
  for mixing with manure.

Easement. Relief.

Eaver. Permanent grass seed.

Edge. Principle, disposition " A good edge."

Eggy-hot. Hot beer, sugar, and eggs.

Elbow-grease. Hard work, or energy in work. " Put
  some elbow grease in it "

Elevener. A slight lunch.

Elleck. A kind of gurnard.

Elmin-tree. The elm-tree.

Ent. To empty, to pour.

Entī! Indeed! " No entī ! "

Enting-down. Raining very heavily, pouring with rain.
  " It's enting down."

Eve, Eave. To thaw, to give with damp or heave.

Evil. A stable-fork with several prongs. " A five-pronged evil."

Evil. A kind of gathering.

Evit, Ebbat. A newt.

Eyeable. Presentable. " That's not very eyeable."

F

Faddy. A rejoicing, a merry making.

Fadgy. Faded, soiled.

Faggied. Devised, planned. " Faggied out a plan."

Faggot. A worthless person ; a term of contempt.

Fairmades, Fairmaids. Cured pilchards, or pilchards prepared for the foreign market

Fairy. A weasel.

Fal-tha-rals. Useless things, trifles.

Fancical. Whimsical, fanciful.

Fang. To receive, to take hold of.

Fanged. " Never fanged to it." Never acknowledged or noticed it.

Fangings. Wages, earnings.

Fay, Fey. Faith.

Feasten. Feast. " Feasten Sunday."

Feather-bog. A bog, a quagmire.

Feather-tye. A feather bed.

Feaps. Pitch and toss.

Fee. Freehold; free. "It's fee land." "He's fee there," *i.e.* welcome to come and go at will.

Feneage. To cheat; to steal; to entice.

Feneaged. Obtained by improper means; enticed. "Feneaged away"

Fescue. A pin or point.

Figs. Raisins.

Figgy-duff. Plum-pudding.

Fine. Very; exceedingly. "Fine and glad to see ee."

Fire-pan. A fire-shovel.

Fit. To prepare, to get ready. "Fit the denner."

Fitch. A polecat.

Fitty. Suitable, proper, nice. "I aint fitty 'tall." "A fitty looking maid."

Flabbergasted. Taken aback. "I was quite flabbergasted."

Flagary. A frolic, a spree.

Flannin. Flannel.

Flat-rod-shaft. A shaft with pumps drawn by horizontal rods, worked by a distant engine or water-wheel.

Flaws. Intermittent showers

Flecktt. A squall of weather, wind or rain.

Flecketts. Flashes, sudden changes of colour, blushes.

Fleeting, Floating. The guttering of candles.

Flesh-meat. Butcher's meat.

Fletters. Rags.

Flew, Flue. A coat of manure spread over land

Flied. Flown

Fligs. Gaudy articles of dress, gaudy attire.

Flink. To throw with a jerk, to toss; to almost accomplish. "Can you say the Lord's prayer, my son?"—"Don't knaw ef I can zactly, sir, but I can gibb'n a brave flink."

Flip. "A flip of the finger." To jerk the finger and thumb.

Flisk. A comb.

Floors. Ground generally paved to deposit minerals or ores for dressing or preparing for sale.

Flop. To spill. "Flopping the water."

Floppervan. An under-petticoat.

Flosh. The dashing of water in, or over, a vessel of any kind.

Floury-milk. A kind of porridge made of flour, milk, and sometimes caraway seeds or currants and spice. (Formerly always given to the workpeople in farm-houses for breakfast on corn-carrying days.)

Floury. Mealy. "Floury potatoes."

Fly-by-night. A racy, thoughtless girl; a gad-about.

Fooright. Forthright, outspoken, straightforward.

Fooch. To push, to shove, etc.; An idea connected with slovenliness.

Fooch. Disorder, confusion.

Fork. To pump dry. "The shaft is in fork."

Forthy. Forward; pert; inquisitive

Fouse, Fauce. To crush, to rumple.

Foused, Fauced. Crushed, rumpled, faded.

Foxing. Deceiving. "He's foxing you."

Foxing-day. A deceitful day, a lull in a storm. "It's only a foxing-day"

Fradge. Dirty, evil-smelling

Fradgan, Fradgeon. An evil-smelling or dirty place ; a receptacle for dirt.

Freath. A hurdle interwoven with boughs, furze, etc.

Freathe. To weave.

Freathed-out. Ragged, ravelled.

French-nuts. Walnuts.

Fringle. An enclosed fire-place or grate capable of generating an intense heat and quickly.

Fringle. A iron crook moving on hinges fastened to the back of an open chimney, on which kettles, etc., are hung.

Fringle-hole. The space under a grate into which the ashes fall.

Froal, F'rall. Although, notwithstanding. (Corruption of *for all*.)

Fuggan. A large bun ; a " plum " bun ; rather heavy baked piece of dough, and often baked with a slice of pork pressed into the top before baking. *See* " Hogan."

Fudgey. " Fudgey-faced." Full-cheeked, fat-faced.

Furzymore. A root of furze.

G

Gabble. To talk noisily ; the chatter of a goose.

Gaddle. To drink greedily.

Gakem. A stupid fellow, a fool.

Gallivanting. Gadding about. " Gallivanting round."

Galore. A large or excessive quantity. " Fish galore."

Galyar. A mad prank.

Galyars. Restive, in a temper.

Gamberns. The hocks of a horse, etc. ; the spreaders on which dead animals are hung.

Gammuts. Sports, games, frolics.

Gard. Gravel, gravelly earth used by housewives for scouring. *See* " Growder."

Garne. A garden.

Gashly. Ghastly, ugly. In some parts of Cornwall used in quite the opposite sense, *i.e.* pretty, good, nice.

Gaver. The cray-fish.

Gays. Sherds, broken china or crockery.

Geek. To peep, to spy, to peer. " I will geek,—I will geek, I tell ee ; while I've the sperit of a man in me I'll geek."

Geeze-dance, Geesedance. A Christmas play, in which the actors are supposed to represent various well-known characters, the principal part being given to Oliver Cromwell.

Gerty. Oatmeal.

Gerrick. The gar-fish *(belone vulgaris)*.

Gick-nor-gack. This nor that, one thing or the other. " He said neither gick-nor-gack."

Gid. The smelt *(osmerus eperlanus)*.

Gidge. An exclamation. " Oh gidge ! "

Ginge. A fine wire fastened round a line just above the hook to prevent fish biting through.

Giss. A saddle girth.

Giss. To girth up.

Gladdie. The yellow-hammer.

Glauze, Glaws. Dried cowdung used for fuel.

Gloas. So spelt in *Williams* "Glow" is coal in *Williams*.

Glaze. To glare. "Glazing at en like a geat guinard"

Gleaney. The guinea-fowl.

Glidder. Polish, shine

Gliddering. Shining, smooth, slippery.

Globical. Unsettled (as applied to weather). "Looking rather globical"

Goad or **Goard.** A pole for measuring land, nine feet long, the off-sett staff.

Glump. To sulk, to be sullen.

Glumping. Sulking.

Go-about. A tramp.

Gone-abroad. Fallen to pieces, dissolved.

Gone-in. Bankrupt, ruined, ended, put a stop to "Gone in ess ee?"

Gone-round-land. Dead; thrown away.

Gone poor. Decayed.

Goodness. The fat used in cooking. "Put plenty of goodness in that paste"

Gook. A sunbonnet.

Goolniggan. A cuttle-rod

Goos. Go. "Goos 'ome," i e go home.

Goosechick. A gosling.

Gorm. To speak in a loud angry voice

Gorming. Speaking loudly, storming.

Goss. Sedge, reeds.

Grafted. Ingrained with dirt.

Grainy. Proud, smart, rather vain.

Grammersow. A milleped

Grass. Surface. (A mining term)

Go the west 'ome. An emphatic way of saying "Go home."

Goosey-gen. A gwidgy-gwee. (St. Just.)

Greep. A trench at the foot of a hedge.

Grey. A badger.

Greybird. The song thrush.

Griddle. A gridiron.

Griddle. To broil, to toast.

Griglans. The dried stalks of heath.

Gripes. Ditches.

Grizzle. To grin broadly, to show the teeth. "Grizzling like a badger."

Groot. Small pieces of dried mud.

Groushams. The dregs of coffee, tea, etc.

Growan. A subsoil of decayed granite.

Growder. Decayed granite, in the form of gravel, used for scouring.

Growts. Dregs.

Grubling. Small, deformed ; emphatically a small cancered apple.

Grute. To clean up a furrow.

Gruter. The breast of a plough.

Guckoos. The blue-bells—wild hyacinths.

Gulge. To drink greedily or quickly.

Gumption. Common sense.

Gurgo, Gurgey. A low turf or stone hedge.

Gurry. A hand-barrow.

Gurt. A shallow ditch or drain.

Gurty-meat. The small entrails of a pig baked with blood, groats, etc.

Gurty-milk. A thin gruel made of milk or water, flour, salt, etc.

Gut-board. The earth board of a plough.

Gweggan. A small shell fish.

Gwidgy-gwee. A small black spot caused by a pinch or bruise.

H

Hack. To dig.

Hackmale, Heckymile. The blue tit.

Hairpitched. With rough, unbrushed coats, such as horses which have been allowed to run wild would have.

Haglan. A haw, the fruit of the hawthorn.

Haglan-tree. The hawthorn.

Hake. Out of proportion, not compact. "A great hake of a house."

Hale. The part of a wooden plough to which the handles, beam and foot were attached.

Hale. The principal room of a house, a parlour.

Half-crease. Half of the increase. Hens are often borrowed to hatch and rear chicken, the owner of the hen receiving half of the brood in payment. Bees, too, are frequently lent and the honey divided.

Hals-nut-hals. The hazel.

Halvens. Halves. "He'll go halvens"

Hames. A straw horse-collar.

Hangbow. The hanging post of a gate.

Happard. A half-pennyworth.

Hapse. To fasten a door or gate, to catch.

Harby-pie. Herb pie.

Harve. A harrow.

Harve, Harvey. To harrow.

Hauves, Auvise, Auvice. The eaves of a house, stack, etc.

Hay. An enclosure. "The church hay."

Hay-maiden. Ground-ivy.

Hailer or **Healer.** A receiver of stolen goods; the encourager of another in wrong-doing. "The healer is as bad as the stealer."

Heap. "Struck all of a heap" Frightened, amazed.

Heapingstock. A stone platform from which horses are mounted.

Heave, Eave. To thaw, to give with damp.

Heavers. Rye-grass.

Heavy-cake. A flat cake made of flour, currants, fat, etc., and usually eaten hot.

Hedgyboar. The hedgehog.

Heel of the hand. The inside of the hand from the thumb to the wrist.

Heep. The hip.

Heggan. A hard, dry cough

Hell. To slate a roof

Heller. A tiler.

Hellins. Slates. " All the hellins blown away."

Hen-chicks. Chicken (as opposed to duck-chicks, *i e.* ducklings).

Het. To heat.

Hetted. Heated. " Hetted brath."

Hetter. A heater.

Hetter. A shackle.

Hetterpin. The pin of a shackle.

Hepse, Haps. The bottom leaf of a door, a half-door

Heva. The cry given by a huer to announce the approach of the pilchard shoals.

Hibbal. A turnip, a knoll, a hummock.

Hibet. The newt.

Hiding. A thrashing. " I'll hide you."

Higgler. An itinerant dealer in butter, eggs, poultry, etc

Hiles, Iles. The beard of barley

Hinge. The liver and lungs of an animal.

Hipped. Depressed in spirits; ill in imagination; hypochondriasis.

Hisk. A wheeze. " Such a hisk "

Hisking. Wheezing.

Hitch. To sew roughly and clumsily. " Hitch en together "

Hobban. *See* HOGGAN.

Hobble. A party of tourists, etc, in charge of a guide or boatman

Hobbler. A ferryman, a guide, a touter

Hobbling. Touting; acting as guide or boatman. " He's gone hobbling "

Hoggan. A heavy cake of flour and currants, raisins or seeds, etc. A flat cake, often cooked with a piece of pork in the centre. " What have you there, my man ?"—" A hoggan." " What's that ? "—" Why a fuggan, to be sure."

Hoise, Hoisey. Hoarse.

Holidays. Parts left untouched in sweeping, dusting, painting, etc. " Plenty of holidays on that door."

Hollensmocks. The sea campion.

Holla-pot. A talkative, empty-headed person.

Hollow-ware. Poultry as opposed to butcher's meat.

Hollow-work. Embroidery.

Holm. The holly.

Holm-screech. The missel-thrush *(turdus viscivorur)*.

Home, Close 'ome. To shut, to fasten. " Close 'ome the door."

Homer. The nearer. " Homer field."

Hoodwood. A forest.

Hoop. The bullfinch.

Hoot. To bray, to cry ; to whistle. " a steamer hooting."

Hooting-cough. Whooping cough.

Hopmass. The medlar.

Hornywink. Poor, desolate. " A hornywink of a thing."

Horse-adder. The dragonfly.

Housen. Houses.

Housin'. Gossiping from house to house.

Hubba. A noise, a disturbance.

Hud. The husks of corn.

Huddicks. Grains of wheat not separated from the husks.

Huffles. The wind huffles.

Huer. The watchman who announces the approach of pilchard shoals, and signals their direction to the men in the seine boats.

Huggo. A sea cave, a cavern.

Hully. A hole in the rocks, often used as a store for shell fish.

Hungry. Stingy, mean.

Hurler. A screen or griddle for sifting corn, etc.

Hurling. A Cornish game, in which the opposing parties try to get and retain possession of a ball, and to carry it into a goal.

Hurling-weather. Drying weather.

Hurry. To frighten.

Hurried. Frightened, worried.

Hurrysome. Hasty, passionate.

Hurts. Wortleberries.

I

Ile. An awn of barley.

Illwish. To bewitch

Impudenter. Saucier, more impudent.

Inchin'. To gradually encroach, to move little by little. "No inchin' there.'

Inkle. Black tape.

Inklemakers. Tapemakers.

Innerds. The inward parts, the bowels.

Insense. To explain, to make clear "Can't be insensed into it."

Inyon. An onion.

Ire. Iron

Iss. Yes. "Iss fie."

Issterday, Essterday. Yesterday.

Ivers! An exclamation. " My ivers ! "

J

Jack Harry's lights. Phantom lights seen to play on the topmasts of ships, and on high places, on dark, stormy nights, warning sailors of the fiercer storm that is bearing down on them.

Jack-o'-lantern. The will-o'-the-wisp *(ignis fatuus)*.

Jacky-ralph. The rock-ray—the rasp

Jail. To walk quickly, to hurry along

Jakes. A state of untidyness.

Jan-jeak, john-jeak. A snail.

Jaunders. The jaundice.

Jaypie. The jay.

Jealous. Suspicious "I had a jealous thoft."

Jellyflower. The gillyflower—the stock.

Jennyquick. A kind of goffering iron.

Jet. To hustle, to push.

Jewish woman. A Jewess.

Jib. To refuse to pull, to be unwilling to start.

Jibs. Small waste bits of cloth.

Jibber. A horse that refuses to pull.

Joan-blunt. A forthright out-spoken woman.

Johnner. A kind of starling.

Johnny-come-fortnight. A travelling draper.

Joram. A large cup; an earthenware vessel. "A geat joram of tay."

Joust. To jolt, to hustle.

Jouster. A hawker of butter, eggs, etc.

Jowdle. To jolt, to shake.

Jowds. Shreds or small pieces. " Boiled to jowds."

Jump. The country.

Just alive. A mining term, used when the ore in a lode can scarcely be seen.

K

Kayher. A sieve.

Kearn. To harden, to fill up.

Kearning. The filling up or hardening of the grain of corn.

Keave. To separate the short straw from thrashed corn.

Keggas. Tall umbelliferous plants.

Keels. Skittles.

Keel-alley. A skittle-alley.

G

Keem. To comb with a small tooth comb.

Keeming-comb. A small tooth comb.

Keenly. A mining term indcating probability of mineral.

Keeping company. Sweethearting, courting.

Keep on. To nag, to reiterate. "Don't keep on so."

Kekezza. A variety of heath *(erica vagans)*.

Kellas. The earth-nut, the common pig-nut.

Kennel. A sty on the eye.

Kew, Cue. An ox shoe; the iron plate on the heel of a boot.

Kex. Dried stalks.

Kibbat. A slap or blow.

Kibbal, Kibble. A bucket for drawing water; an iron bucket for drawing ore, rubbish, water, etc., from mines.

Kibbing. Repairing fences.

Kicklish. In an unstaple position, risky, unsteady, easily overt-turned. "A kicklish sort of a thing."

Kiddlywink, Tiddlywink. A beershop.

Kidge. To stick together (as a broken bone), to adhere.

Kieve. A large tub.

Killiars. Rough, ferny ground.

Killick, Kellick. A grapple used as an anchor for boats.

Kit. The buzzard or kite.

Kit. Kindred, crew, gang. "The whole kit."

Kittens. The kidneys.

Kittereen. A van, a rude kind of omnibus.

Kitey. Flighty, undependable.

Kitting. Stealing. (A mining term—purloining ore underground.)

Kittybags. Coarse pieces of cloth, or straw bands used as leggings.

Kiskan. A small sheaf of corn.

Kiskey. Brittle; the dry stalk of umbelliferous plants; the thistle.

Klidgy, Clidgy. Sticky, viscous, adhesive.

Klop. To walk lame.

Knack. To stop working. " The bal's knacked."

Knacking. A handkerchief.

Knap. The top of the hill.

Knuckle-in. To give in, to submit. " Don't you knuckle in to him,"

Knick. To cheat, to deceive, to outdo.

Kowks. The feet (in contempt). " Great kowks."

Kybosh. Affectation, display, pretence.

L

Labbat. The ear. " I'll pull your labbats."

Labbat. An inferior labourer ; an attendant on others.

Lace. A measure of land—18 feet square. Local—rod, pole, or perch.

Lace. To thrash, to beat.

Lacing. A thrashing.

Lace-ups. Laced boots. " Put on your lace-ups."

Lag. To bedraggle, to plaster in mud.

Lagged. Dress covered with mud ; to have the garments covered with mud.

Lamb's-tails. The willow blossom.

Lambswool. A drink made of hot milk, eggs, sugar, and nutmeg.

Lank. Loose.

Lanky. Overgrown, long and thin.

Lap. To beat.

Lap. Wet, muddy clothing left about the house. "A lot of dirty lap."

Lappior. A dancer; a miner who dresses the refuse ores that are left.

Lask. A thin slip of fish used as bait.

Lasking. Keeping close into land.

Lash. To pour, to rain heavily; to throw with force. "Lashing down."

Lashings. Plenty, a large quantity.

Latten, Lattice. Tin, tinware.

Lattice-pan. A tin pan.

Launder. A conduit of iron or wood to carry off water from the roofs of houses.

Leary. Hungry, weak and faint from hunger; empty, void. (It is a mining term for the spare underground from which the mineral has been removed.)

Lease. To pick stones off land; to gather, to glean.

Lease-cattle. Cattle not yet turned to fatten, milkless cows.

Leasing-stones. Small stones gathered from the land.

Leat. A small river, a stream.

Leatherwing. The bat.

Leave. To let. "I'll leave you knaw." "Leave me go."

Leggas. Legs.

Lem. An imp, a rogue, when used of a person. (Probably a corruption of "limb of the devil.")

Lem. Feature. "His face is his best lem."

Lemon-plant. The verbena.

Lent-lily. The daffodil.

Lerrup. A blow; to thrash.

Lerrup. An untidy person, a slattern.

Lerrups. Rags, pieces. "Torn to lerrups."

Let. To hinder, hindrance. "More haste, more let"

Letterpooch, Letterputch. A slattern, an untidy person; also a kind of dance.

Levan, Leaven. Fermented dough used in barley bread instead of yeast; the leavan of Scripture.

Lew, Lewth. Shelter; out of the wind.

Liard. A liar.

Lichway. The way by which a corpse is carried to church.

Lick. A scrape, a hasty wipe over.

Lick-and-a-promise. Carelessly done. "Give un a lick-and-a-promise," *i.e.* finish off anyhow now, with a promise for better work next time.

Licks. Leeks.

Licky-pie. A pie of leeks, pork, etc.

Lidden. An old tale, a repitition of abuse, etc. "No more of your lidden."

Lie. To subside, beaten down. "The wind has gone to lie." "The corn has gone to lie."

Lights. The lungs.

Likely. Tall; well-formed.

Likes. Possibility, probability. "Any likes of their coming."

Like-a-thing. As it were, as one may say.

Lime-ash. A sort of cement used for flooring. "A lime-ash floor."

Lime-kill. A lime-kiln.

Linnick. A linnet.

Linhay. A shed with a roof but no sides ; a cattle-shed.

Lintern. A lintel.

Linuth. Kidney.

Linuth-duff. Kidney pudding.

Lipsy. To lisp. "She speaks lipsy."

Listing. The selvage of flannel, etc. ; the coloured stripes on a blanket.

Lisamoo, Lizzamoo. The cow-parsnip.

Littlemount. A game of bat and ball, a sort of " rounders," which was always played on St. Michael's Mount on Easter Mondays by the whole of the inhabitants, young and old.

Loady-apple. A double apple.

Loagy. Dull, slow, heavy in gait.

Lobb. To wean a calf.

Locust. A sweet made of treacle.

Lodger (Newlyn). A vessel moored off in the lake is spoken of as " out in the lodger."

Log. To rock, to move to and fro.

Logan-rock. A rock capable of being rocked.

Long-cripple. A viper, a snake.

Looch. The short straw, chaff, etc., from thrashing ; refuse.

Lords-and-ladies. The *arum maculatum*.

Lougy. Slow in movement, heavy.

Louster. To work hard, to labour. " My man can't louster." " He that can't schemy must louster."

Loustering. Big, able to work. " A great loustering girl."

Loustering-work. Hard, heavy work

Love-entangle. The flannel-flower.

Lubber-cock. Turkey cock ; also a term of contempt· " A great lubber-cock."

Lubber-headed fool. A simpleton.

Lucky-bone. The knuckle-bone of a leg of mutton, used sometimes as a charm.

Lug. A worm found in sea-sand.

Lugg. Grass and weeds in corn.

Lump. To bear, to put up with, to be resigned. " If you don't like it, you can lump it."

Lurgy. A fit of laziness. " He's got the lurgy."

Lyners. Small bundles of reed.

M

Mabyers. Young hens.

Maggots. Fancies, ideas.

Maggot. A magpie

Mait. To feed. " Have ee maited the pigs ? "

Make-out. To put out, to pretend.

Make-wise. To pretend, to make-believe.

Malkin. A slattern ; a rag mop used for cleaning ovens.

Mallygolder. A large jelly-fish.

Man-engine. A machine by which miners ascend and descend the shafts of deep mines.

Manshons. Small loaves baked without tins.

Margay-soup. Soup of a kind of dog-fish, parsley, etc.

Marinade. To marinate, to pickle.

Marsel, Morsel. A slice of bread and butter.

Mashes. A large quantity, a great deal.

Maun, Maund. A hamper, a large basket.

May. The blossom of the hawthorn.

May-bird. The whimbrel.

Maygam, May-game. Fun, frolic; to make a butt of. "I won't be made a May-game by them."

Mazed. Mad, cracked-brained. "Mazed as a curly."

Mazed-getty-puttick, Maze-gerry-pattrick. A wild harum-scarum fellow.

Mazlin, Mazzlin. Silly, bewildered. "Scat un mazzlin."

Meader. A mouse.

Meader. A mower.

Meat-earth. The surface soil.

Meggyhowler, Meggahowler. A large night moth.

Meezy-y-mazy. Muddled, confused, bewildered ; a game.

Melt. The soft roe of fishes.

Merl. The link of a chain

Merry-dancers. The northern lights *(aurora borealis)*

Merryman. A clown.

Metheglin. A drink made from honey, etc.

Mews. Moss.

Minch, Minchy. To play truant.

Mingle-com-por. Confusion, discord, muddle.

Milchy. The flour from sprouted corn.

Milky-disel, Milky-dizle. The thistle.

Milyer. The hinge of a door or gate which works with a pin in a stone; axle or pivot on which a wheel or roller turns.

Miserable. Miserly.

Miracle-play. A farce, a drama. "A regular miracle-play."

Miss-the-hand. To make a mistake, to blunder. "Missed her hand there."

Mocket. The bib of an apron.

Moile. A mule.

Molly-caudle. An effeminate man.

Monger. A horse collar made of twisted straw.

Moole. To knead bread.

Moonshine. Smuggled brandy.

Moorstone. Granite.

Mops-and-brooms. Disorder, sixes and sevens; muddled with drink.

Mopse. A bridle with blinkers.

Moppey-heedy. Hide and seek.

More, Maur. A root.

More-and-moold. Root and branch.

Mort, Mart. Lard

Morrops. Sheep-runs near the sea.

Mot, Mote. The stump of a tree, etc.

Mother. A fungus which forms in fluids, such as vinegar, cider, etc.

Mother-margets, Mother-margeys. The bluebottle
  fly.

Mow. A stack.

Mowhay. The yard in which the ricks are placed.

Muck. Filth.

Muck. Pounded apples.

Muggard. The mugwort.

Muggets. Entrails.

Mulligrubs. The colic.

Mully. The bull-head *(cottus gobio)*.

Mumper. A tramp, a beggar.

Mun. Rotten fish used as manure.

Munge. To chew.

Murfles. Freckles, spots on the skin.

Mur. A sea-fowl (the puffin).

Murphy. A potato.

Muryans. Ants.

Music-man. A musician.

Mutting. Sulky, sulking.

N

Nack. "A nawble nack too." A noble thing too, a
  trifle not worth mentioning (spoken ironically).

Nackin. A handkerchief.

Nailspring. A small splinter of skin at the root or side
  of a finger nail.

Nan? Anan? What do you say ?

Name up. Noted, famed, to be talked about " Her name's up for that."

Narry one. Not one.

Nashed. Afflicted, weak in body, sickly.

Nattlings. Pigs' entrails

Neap. A turnip.

Near. Miserly.

Neck. The last sheaf of wheat cut in the harvest.

Neck. " To cry the neck." An old ceremony which took place at the end of the wheat cutting, when the principal harvester (or man with the loudest voice), the rest of the work-people standing round, took the " neck," and swinging it from the shoulder to the ground, cried :—

　　" I have en ! I have en ! I have en ! "

Another answers ·—

　　" What have ee? what have ee? what have ee?"

Then the first :—

　　" A neck ! a neck ! a neck ! "

Then all together :—

　　" Hoora ! hoora ! hoora ! "

This was usually repeated three times, and then the " neck " was hung up in the farm house kitchen until Christmas Eve, when it was given to the best ox in the stall.

Neck of the foot. The instep.

Nekegga. A kind of heath, probably *callum vulgaris.*

Nessle-bird. The youngest or smallest in the nest; the youngest of a family.

New-vangs. New fancies or ideas.

Nice-chance. A narrow escape, just missed. " Nice chance that wasn't scat."

Nick. To tick. " The clock's nicking loudly."

Nick. To deceive, to take in.

Niddle, Niddil. A needle.

Niff. A temper, a pet.

Niffed. To be in a pet, offended, sulky.

Niflin, Newflin. Newfoundland cod.

Night-crow. A term applied to children who stay up late at nights. " A regular night-crow."

Night-rear. A nightcap.

Noggle-head. A simpleton.

No fool behind the door. Not easily duped. " He's no fool behind the door."

Nonce, Nouse. To act designedly, on purpose.

No speak. Silence, no answer.

Nose-warmer. A short clay pipe.

Nort. Nothing.

Nosey. Saucy, interfering.

Nub. A lump. " A nub of coal."

Nuddick. The nape of the neck.

Nut-hals. The hazel.

Nyst, Nist. Near by, close to.

O

Oak-web. A cockchaffer.

Oar-weed. Sea-weed.

Odds, no odds. No difference.

Off one's chump. Mad, insane.

Oiler. A waterproof, such as is used by fishermen.

Old men's bucks. Old mine workings.

Ollick, Hollick. A kind of leek.

Owner's 'count. A meeting of the shareholders or adventurers of a mine and the mine agents to consider or audit their accounts.

Ope. Opening.

Ore-dresser. One who is thoroughly acquainted with the methods of separating and cleaning ores.

Organ. The herb pennyroyal.

Orts. Fragments.

Outlander. A foreigner.

Out of core. Working in one's spare time.

Overlook. To bewitch.

Over run the constable. Gone in debt, come to the end of one's resources.

Overgone. Excited, carried away with delight.

Ozle, Uzzle, Ouzle. The windpipe

P

Paddylincum. The small boneless squid.

Padgypaow. A lizard.

Paens. Parsnips.

Palched. Of weak or broken constitution, a valetudinarian.

Pallace. A cellar used for the balking of pilchards.

Pancrack. An earthenware vessel, a small pan.

Panshon. A milk-pan.

Pare. A gang or company of men working at the same thing, a detachment, a set of things.

Parrick. A small coarse earthenware jug.

Parson-in-the-pulpit. The cuckoo-pint *(arum maculatum)*.

Pass. A beating, a stripe, a punishment.

Passage. A ferry.

Passel. A large number, a quantity.

Passy. *Et cetera.*

Patchook. A billhook.

Pattick, Paddick. A stupid, senseless person.

Papishers. Papists.

Pea. The hard roe in fishes.

Peart. Lively.

Peath. A draw-well.

Peaze. To weigh.

Pednans. Pieces, parts.

Pedn-pral. A horse's head.

Pedn-paley. The tom-tit.

Peeny. Musty (applied to stale meats).

Pellas, Pelaz. The naked oats, the *avena nuda* of Ray.

Peltering. Pelting, pouring down (as of rain),

Pennard. A pennyworth.

Pennyleggan. Penniless.

Penny short. Not too wise.

Pernic, Pernick. Precise, stiff in manner, prim, neat.

Pervans. Frayed edges.

Piddlymean, Pednamene. Head to foot; two or more articles lying side by side the reverse way.

Piff. To offend, to vex.

Piggywidden. The smallest of the litter, the youngest of a family. *See* " Nestle-bird."

Pig's-crow. A pigsty.

Pilcher. A pilchard.

Piler. An instrument of crossed iron used for beating off the ears of barley from the grain.

Pilf. Dry stubble; filmy dust.

Pillyer. A hummock or small heathy knoll like an ant-hill, found in light uncultivated land.

Pilm. Light fibrous dust or down

Pilmer. A downpour of rain.

Pinbone. The hip.

Pindy meat. Tainted meat

Pinnick. The wryneck (attendant on the cuckoo).

Pip. A disease common to fowls

Pipped. Offended, vexed

Piskey. A fairy.

Piskey-led. Bewildered, perplexed, led away by the fairies.

Piskey-ridden. The nightmare.

Piskeystool. A mushroom.

Pitch. To pave. (A mining term.)

Pitch-haired. With a rough uncombed coat, as horses which are allowed to run wild.

Pitch-to. To set to work earnestly.

Pitch up to. To make advances.

Pitwork. Mining machinery placed in the shafts to draw the water from below.

Planchin. A wooden floor.

Plat. A level place.

Plat down. To smooth, to press down.

Plat-footed. Flat-footed.

Please? What do you say?

Please sure. Decidedly, really. " Yes, please sure."

Plethon. To plait, to braid.

Plisher. A branch that has been bent down and fastened with crooks.

Plosh. A wet, miry place.

Plosher. A young bream.

Ploshy. Wet, miry.

Pluff. Spongy, soft, tough.

Plum. To ferment dough, to rise. " The bread is plum," _i.e._ ready for the oven.

Plum. Soft, crackbrained.

Pluman. A plum.

Plump. A draw-well.

Poam. To thump, to beat.

Pock. A shove.

Poddlin round. Doing odd jobs; working aimlessly; meddling.

Podger. A small coarse earthenware vessel, a platter.

Podgy. Short, stumpy.

Polan. A salt water pool.

Pook. A cock of hay or turf.

Poot. A kick like a horse, a push with the foot.

Pop-an-towse. Fuss, an uproar.

Pop-dock. The foxglove.

Por, Pore. A fuss, a temper, a rage.

Poss-up. To support, to prop-up, to lean against. " Possed-up with pillows."

Pound. A cider mill.

Powdered. Slightly salted, corned.

Powers. A great deal, a quantity.

Prall. To attach tin pans, kettles, etc., to the tail of an animal,—or cards, bits of paper, etc., to persons' coats.

Praze, Prase. A small common.

Preedy. Pert, precocious; conceited, forward.

Prink. To pleat.

Prinky. Attentive to dress, spruce, natty.

Prinking-along. Walking daintily or affectedly.

Pritchell. A heath stem or other article used to stick in the wick of a chill (lamp) to prevent its falling back into the oil; the pointed piece of iron used by a smith to stick in the nail-hole of a horse-shoe for the purpose of holding it to the hoof.

H

Project. An experiment.

Progue. To prod.

Prong. A silver fork.

Proper. Handsome.

Proud-flesh. Inflamed flesh.

Prove. To thrive.

Punyon. The angle of a roof, a gable.

Punyon end. The gable end.

Pure. In good health.

Pure. Simple, unpretentious. " A pure little sermon."

Purvan. The pith of the rush, used as wicks.

Purgy. Short, stumpy.

Put. To take. " Put it away."

Put-going. Murdered.

Put the miller's eye out. To mix too much water with
dough in cooking, or with the spirit in grog.

Puzzle-headed spoons. Apostle spoons.

Q

Quail. To fade, to wither.

Quailaway. A sty on the eyelid.

Qualker. A hard fall. " I threw him a regular qualker."

Quam. A qualm, a fainting fit.

Quarry. A pane of glass.

Quat. To squat, to flop down ; to hide away.

Queel. To wriggle, to coil, to twist.

Quellat, Quillet. A small field or enclosure.

Queens. Scallops.

Queer. Beds or layers of ground. (A mining term.)

Queock. The horn of a bullock's hoof, often used by miners for pouring water into the holes they are boring.

Quilkin. A frog.

Quirkish. Jocose.

Quilter. To beat, to thrash.

R

Rab. Hard, gravelly ground.

Rabble-rout. A noisy mob.

Rabbet et! "Odd rabbet et!" Bother! confound it !

Race. A strand or string (of onions chiefly), a row of things.

Radjall. A loose heap of large stones, such as waste from a quarry.

Rag, Ragging. The blowing of the wind before rain. "Ragging for rain."   .

Ramping. Raging.

Ramping and Roving. Raving, approaching lunacy.

Ran. A wren.

Ran-dan. Gadding about. "Always upon the ran-dan."

Randigal. A rigmarole, a nonsensical, unconnected story.

Randyvooze. Confusion; riot; also a place of meeting. (French, *rendez-vous*.)

Ranters. Early Primitive Methodists.

Rare, Rear. Early.

Rare-mouse. The bat.

Rash. Brittle, crisp.

Ratlan. Fallow.

Ratlan field. A fallow field.

Raw milk. New unskimmed milk.

Raw ream. Cream from milk that has not been scalded.

Raw head. *See* RAW REAM.

Rawnish. Hungry, ravenous.

Ream. To separate the cream from milk.

Ream. To stretch.

Reamer. A skimmer.

Reese. To beat out corn.

Reese. The falling of grain from the ears of corn, the falling out of grain.

Regrator. An itinerant dealer in poultry, etc.; a hawker.

Rescan, Ruskin. A small stack or rick of reed.

Riders. A circus.

Riffled. Roofs unslated by a storm, uncovered.

Rig. A frolic, a noise.

Riggle, Riddle. To clear or stir up the fire. "Riddle out the grate."

Roadling, Roodling. Wandering in mind, delirious.

Roker. A cheat.

Ropy. Applied to flour that has lost its freshness and has been injured by damp, but more correctly applied to the bread made from such flour ; stringy.

Rory-tory. Conspicuously smart or gay ; tawdry.

Rouging. Lifting with difficulty, violent labour.

Rouse. A rattling noise.

Roving. Raving.

Rows. Refuse from ore, which refuse has not yet had its tin separated from it.

Row-tin. The mineral ore or black tin which has been separated from the rows

Rubbage. Rubbish, refuse.

Rummage. Confusion, a disorder. " What a rummage the room is in."

Ruddick. The wooden beam across a cart which acts as a hinge on which it is tilted.

Rull. To roll corn into sheaves ready for the binders.

Rummet. Dandruff.

Rumped-up. Drawn together with cold

Rumpy. Uneven.

Run. A landslip.

Runner. A round towel placed on a roller, usually placed behind kitchen doors.

Running wound. A wound from which matter is continually discharged.

Rusking-comb. A large tooth comb.

S

Sam. To partially dry. "To bake in a sam oven," *i.e.* to bake in a partially heated oven.

Sampson. A drink made of brandy, cider, and sugar, with a little water.

Sampson with his hair on. Sampson made with a double quantity of brandy.

Sam-sawdled. Not well cooked, only partly ready.

Sappy. Silly, not wise.

Saund-sleeper, Seven-sleeper. The Buanet moth.

Save-all. A pinafore, an apron.

Sawan. A cave at the bottom of a cliff.

Sawdle. To cook too slowly, to simmer.

Sawdled. Sodden, imperfectly cooked.

Sawg. A stump

Scall. A scale of ground.

Scaow, Scow. The elder tree.

Scat. To break ; to knock ; to slap.

Scat. A blow. " A scat in the chacks."

Scat. Ruined, bankrupt. "Gone scat."

Scat. A season, a spell. "A scat of dryth."

Scaunse. Sense.

Scavell-an-gow, Skavelling-gow. "The bench of lies." Rag-tag and bob-tail, riff-raff.

School. A shoal of fish.

Sclum. To scratch.

Scollops. Greaves.

Scoot. To rush away, to hurry.

Scoot-a-paw, Scutapaw. A flat shallow-bottomed boat.

Scopious. Copious, plentiful. " Without scopious showers and harmonial dews we can't grow anything."

Scouring-geaard. Decomposed granite used for scouring.

Scramming. Searching about for what can be picked up.

Scranch. To crunch.

Scrawed. Scorched, dried up, withered.

Screech. A quick blaze or fire of heath or furze

Screw. The shrew mouse.

Scriff. To draw together with cold, to stoop over the fire ; to nestle for shelter from the cold

Scriff-scraff. The refuse, or cast-off bits.

Scrimp. To pinch, to give meagre quantity.

Scrimpin. Meagre, miserly.

Scrinked. Screwed up, wrinkled.

Scroached, Scrolled, Scrowled. Scorched, broiled.

Scroff. Refuse, small potatoes, etc

Scroff. The foam of the sea.

Scrolls. Greaves

Scrovey. Mean.

Scrow. To scratch.

Scrowlers. Broiled pilchards

Scruff. The nape of the neck. " Got en by the scruff."

Scruff. To take hold of, to pull about ; to fight

Scrump. To hump the shoulders.

Scud. To spill, to scatter, to spread.

Scuddy-ground. Rough, uneven ground.

Scudmore. Small pieces of floating wreckage; drift-wood. "I saw a vessel strike the Cowlow; she scat all to scudmore, and the broushans came ashore in the cove."

Scuffle. To work the soil with a "cultivator."

Scur. To scratch.

Scute. The iron on the heel of a boot or shoe.

Sem. To appear, to seem.

Seame. A horse load.

Seed. Saw.

Seyme. Melted fat, grease. "Goose seyme."

Shallal-band. A band of persons with tin kettles, pans, etc., to ironically serenade newly-married couples.

Shally-go-naked. A flimsy article of dress — (from "shall I go naked?)—suggesting that the garment is a compromise between wearing something or nothing.

Shape. Disorder, confusion, condition. "A pretty shape he's in, I can tell ee."

Shave your head and go east. A contemptuous phrase, possibly referring to the time when it was the custom to go on pilgrimages.

Shedrick. "That gate was a shedrick." Delapidated.

Sherds. Pieces of broken pottery.

Sherming. Big, large.

Shern. A cream dish.

> "Here's a fern
> To measure your shern;
> Please give us a mossel of bread and cream."

A May-day song, when parties of children visited the farm houses, bringing with them ferns to measure the cream dish. If one was big enough to go round the dish, bread and cream was given.

Shevver. The bar of a gate.

Shevver. The sheath of an oven

Shig, Shug. To cheat or trick in games or in play.

Shimshanking. Mean, shuffling.

Shine. Uproar, row, fuss, stir. "Never seed such a shine in your life."

Shiner. An occasional sweetheart.

Shoal. To sponge or hang on to others.

Shoaler. A person who sponges on others.

Shoaling. Imposing on good nature, sponging

Shot. A species of trout.

Showl. A shovel.

Shrim. A cold shiver, a chill.

Shrump. To shrug.

Shute. A stream of water.

Skeat. "A skeat of rain." A heavy fall of rain.

Skeat. A rent, a rag, to tear.

Skedgewith. The privet.

Skeet. To squirt water, to syringe "Skeet the winders."

Skeeter. A syringe.

Skever. A skewer.

Skew, Skiff. A slight driving shower, driving misty rain.

Skibbat, Skivet. A small compartment in a chest.

Skitter. To make ducks and drakes on water; to slide.

Skittery. Slippery.

Skrim. To shiver with cold.

Skrinked. Wrinkled up, screwed.

Skrum. *See* SKRIM.

Skuffler. A "cultivator."

Skurge, Scourge. To touch obliquely, a light oblique touch, to glance against anything.

Skute, Scute. The iron on the heel of a boot or shoe.

Slaggy. Wet, miry.

Slaw-cripple. The slow-worm.

Slawterpooch. An ungainly, slovenly person.

Slew. To turn on one side, to twist around. " She slewed 'round."

Slewed. Intoxicated.

Sliddery. Slippery. " Sliddery quay."

Slide. A sledge.

Slights. " In his slights." Partly dressed, not fully clothed.

Slinger. A jobber.

Slips. Young pigs.

Slivers. Pieces.

Slock. To entice, to draw away, to lead astray.

Slocum. A slow, heavy person, an idler.

Slone. The sloe.

Slooch. To scrape the feet in walking, to drag. " Slooching along."

Sloot. To scrape or drag the feet.

Slooge. Fine dust caused by the working of a drill.

Sloots. Old shoes or slippers.

Slotter. To spill about.

Slottery. Damp, muddy weather.

Slump. An unskilled, careless worker.

Small people The fairies

Smead. The pole of a scythe.

Smeech. A strong disagreeable smell caused by burning rags, etc.

Smeet. To snigger, to laugh, to giggle.

Smudder. A cloud of smoke or dust

Smulk. A dirty, disagreeable person.

Snodderwig. A black beetle. " Granny, plummans got leggas ?" " No, cheeld vean !" " Then I've been and clunked a snodderwig."

Snowl. To loudly crunch or chew.

Soase. Colloquial expression equivalent to saying " friends, folks, companions," etc., as " come soase," " yes soase " (probably from the Latin *socius*, companion).

Sodger. A red herring.

Sog. The fitful sleep or unconsciousness of a person in sickness.

Soursop. The sorrel.—Soursops and nettles were reckoned great dainties with children.

Spal, Spaal. To fine for loss of time.

Spalled. Fined for loss of time.

Spall. To break stones or minerals.

Spalls. Fragments of stone or metal.

Spalling. Breaking stones or ore

Spalling-hammer. A small sledge for breaking stones, etc.

Span. A tether, a fetter.

Span. To tether.

Sparbles. Sparables

Sparble-pie. A kick (from a sparable boot).

Spare. A term applied to work which ill repays the time and labour bestowed on it.

Spar-stone. Granite.

Sparr. To disagree, to nag, to argue

Spell. To throw out hints toward an end.

Spelling. Hinting, using means to obtain.

Spicketty. Speckled. "A spicketty hen."

Spiff. Smart, dressy. " Looking spiff."

Spiffy. Rather grand, spicy, stuck-up, showy. " A spiffy old dear."

Spinning-drone. The cockchafer.

Spence. A cupboard under a stairs.

Spit. To cut up the top soil with a shovel; the top soil to the depth of a shovel.

Splat. A plot of ground. " The green splat."

Splatty. Bespattered, spotted.

Splitting along. Hurrying.

Sprall. To fetter.

Spraggly. An irregular pattern, an uneven design. " All spraggly like "

Sprawl. Energy. " Hardly sprawl to move along."

Sprawls. A disease common to young ducks and chicken.

Spray. To roughen, to chap.

Sprayed. Chapped with the wind, roughened.

Spronncy. Lively, jolly, excited.

Sprouncing. Walking heavily, stamping.

Spud. A troublesome child.

Spuds. Potatoes.

Spur. A spell of work.

Spurt, Sput. Temper, rage. "In a spurt"

Sputter. To stammer with rage.

Squabba. Small pieces. "Scat all to squabba."

Squab-pie. A pie of apples, onions, meat, raisins, etc.

Squarde. To tear, to rend.

Squard. A rent or tear.

Squat. To eat immoderately.

Squinney. To squint, to turn the eyes, to look athwart

Squinsey. The quinsey.

Squitches. Jerks, jumps. "She's got the squitches."

Stag. To stick in the mud, to be over shoes in the mud.

Stain, Stean. A coarse earthenware vessel.

Stank. To tread heavily; to stamp

Stank. A bad scrape or condition.

Stare. A starling.

Stary-gazy-pie, Gazy-pie. Pilchard-pie with the heads of the fish showing through the crust.

Stave. To thrust, to strike.

Stave. To walk quickly, to hurry along.

Staver. An energetic, go-ahead person

Stayed, Staid. Aged.

Steeve. A draught of wind.

Steeve. To be chilled, to be nearly frozen. "Steeved with the wind."

Stem. A day's work.

Steppons, Stippons. Stone steps.

Stew. A fuss, rage.

Stich in the side. A sharp sudden pain occasioned by fast running or walking.

Stickings, Strickings. The last drops of a cow's milk.

Stillwaters. Distilled peppermint water. (A favourite remedy.)

Stiracoose. A bustling woman.

Stock. "Christmas stock." The yule log.

Stounds. Sharp shooting pains. "Stounds in the head."

Strake. To sweep lightly and carelessly ; to stray.

Strake. An appliance for cleaning ore.

Straking. Straying, wandering about.

Stram. A loud noise.

Stram. To run heedlessly ; to slam.

Stramming. Exaggerated. "A stramming great lie ; a "stramming great bonnet."

Strange. Queer, crazy.

Strat. To abort.

Stroath. To walk quickly ; to hurry.

Stroath. "A regular stroath for work." A quick worker.

Stroil. Couch grass.

Stroll. A confused mass of rubbish.

Strollop. A slattern, an untidy person.

Strop. A cord, a piece of string.

Strove. To argue obstinately. "He strove me down."

Strub. To rob a bird's nest ; to glean apples after the crop has been removed.

St. Tibb's Eve. An imaginary time. "I'll do it St. Tibb's Eve, neither before nor after Christmas.

Stuan. A blow.

Stub. To dig up stumps or roots of trees, etc.

Stub. A stump.

Studdle. The stall-post for cattle.

Stuggy. Thick-set, short and stout.

Sturridge. Uproar, confusion.

Sturt, Start. Progress, gain.

Suant. Even, smooth ; to spread evenly.

Suchy-meat. A pudding made of small entrails, blood, barley, etc.

Sue. To go dry from milk. "The cow is gone to sue."

Sumpmen. Men who work at sinking mine shafts.

Sunbeam. The gossamer.

Sure 'nough. Certainly, truly.

Survey. An auction.

Swabstick. A mining implement for cleaning a hole, etc.

Swaise. To wave or swing the hands.

Swaising. Swinging the arms.

Swap. The gadfly.

Sweeled. Singed. "A sweeled cat."

Swogger. To swagger, to boast ; a scolding

Swinging. Large, heavy.

T

Tabs. Dried cowdung used as manure.

Table-board. A table.

Tack, Tackle. To harness.

Tack. To slap or stroke with the open hand.

Taffle. To entangle.

Tags. Narcissi. (Mount.)

Tail-corn. Small, withered grain.

Tail-pipe. To attach kettles or pans, etc., to an animal s tail. *See* PRALL.

Take. Worry, fuss. " A pretty take."

Taken on the ground hop. To be taken by surprise ; at a disadvantage

Talfat. A garret, an open bedroom.

Tamlin. A miner's tool.

Tamping. Materials used to compress the explosive used in blasting rock, etc.

Tamping-iron. An implement, stick, etc. (should be of hard wood or copper), used for ramming the tamping into the holes drilled for blasting.

Tang. An unpleasant taste

Tantrums. Anger, rage, ill-temper.

Tap. To sole a boot or shoe ; the sole of a boot or shoe.

Tarry. To struggle to get free.

Tatchy. Teasy, irritable.

Tatie-rattle. A stew.

Team. To dip up.

Team. To lade from one vessel to another.

Tear. A rage, fuss, storm.

Teel. To plant, to till, to set.

Teeled. Buried, planted.

Teen. To light.

Temper. Moisture in the soil.

Tend. To wait on others ; to supply.

Tender. A waiter.

Tender. Uncertain.—Applied to weather, as " the sky is looking tender," *i.e.* unsettled.

Tescan. A small bundle of corn gathered by reapers.

Thicky-there. That one.

The out of it. The end, the finish.

Thoft. Thought.

Thrashel. A flail.

Thumbinds. Straw ropes used as leggings. So named from being twisted and first coiled round the thumb.

Thunder and lightning. Bread and cream and treacle.

Thunder-planet. A thunder sky.

Thurl. Thin, hollow, lean.

Thurt-eyed. Cross-eyed.

Tidden. Tender, sensitive

Tiddly-wink, Kiddly-wink. A beer-shop.

Tiff. To drink from a bottle.

Tiffed. Vexed, sullen.

Tiflings. Short ends of cotton, or very small shreds left from sewing ; separate fibres of cloth.

Tied. A horse " boggled."

Tigga, Tegga. To touch ; also a game.

Tight. Drunk.

Timmersome. Fearful, nervous.

Timbering-hill. The staircase.

Tinged-up. Hung up, tied up.

Tingler. A bell.

Tinners. Miners.

Titivate. To put in order, to smarten.

I

Toad-in-the-hole. A piece of fat meat baked with a crust round it.

To and again. From time to time, off and on.

Toit. Off-handed, proud, stiff.

Tom-holla. A rowdy person.

Tom-toddy. A tadpole.

Tom-taylor. The " daddy-longlegs."

Tongue. To scold, to abuse.

Tongue-pad. A chatterbox.

Toothpuller. A quack dentist.

Top-dress. To manure on the surface of the land.

Top-dressing. Surface manure.

Tor. Light turfy soil. "Tor" in Celtic Cornish is "a prominence," " the swell of a mountain," a mountain."

Totalish. Silly, imbecile.

Touble. A double-pointed pickaxe.

Touch-pipe. A short interval for rest in the midst of work.

Towan. A sandy hillock or dune.

Town, Townplace. A farmyard.

Towse. Fuss, uproar. " Pop and towse."

Towser. A coarse apron.

Trade. Anything of not much account. (Often applied to doctor's medicine.)

Trapse. To walk.

Trapsing. Wandering about, gadding.

Travish. To wander over, to walk aimlessly. (Corruption of *traverse.*)

Treag, Trig. Small shell-fish, such as limpets, periwinkles, etc. "Trig" in Celtic Cornish is " ebbing of the sea."

Troach. To hawk goods.

Troach. To tread under foot, to trample.

Troachers. Hawkers or pedlars.

Troll-foot. A club-foot, a foot turned inwards.

Troytown. Disorder, confusion.

Truff. Trout.

Trug. To jog along.

Trug. A hard worker. " A good trug."

Tub. A species of gurnard.

Tubban. A clod of earth, turf, etc.

Tucker. A lace frill or collar.

Tucking. An operation in seining, by which the net is gradually drawn together.

Tuck-net. The net used in tucking.

Tummals. A quantity.—Often applied to the quantity of straw in a crop of corn. " Good tummals," *i.e.* a good crop of corn.

Tunaggle. The fastener of a gate.

Tuntree. The pole of an ox cart.

Turmut. A turnip.

Tut. A hassock, a footstool.

Tut-work. Piece-work.

Twadden. It was not.

Twick. A sharp pull or jerk, to snatch.

Twingle. To wriggle, to squirm.

Two-handed-fellow. A clumsy workman.

Tye, Bed-tye. A feather bed. " Ty " in Celtic Cornish " to cover," to roof," " to thatch."

U

Ugly. Cross, poor-tempered, wicked.

Uncle. A term used in addressing any old man—not necessarily a relative. (In common use in Cornwall and Spain.)

Unbeknown. Not known, not acquainted.

Underground Cappen. An overseer (captain) of the work being done underground in mines.

Underheed. Private, underhand.

Unream. To skim cream from milk.

Unrip. To rip.

Uprise. To church women.

Upscud. To spill, to upset.

Urge. To retch.

Uzzle. The " Adam's apple " in the throat ; the windpipe.

V

Vally. Value.

Varying. Sheet lightning ; St. Elmo's fire.

Vean. Little " Cheel vean," *i.e.* " little child." (Often used as a term of endearment.)

Vear. Barren, unfruitful.

Vear, Veer. A sucking pig, a young pig.

Vermut. Vermin.

Veor. Great.

Vestry. The smiling of sleeping infants. "In the vestries."

Vinid. Green mould, mouldy

Visgey. A sort of pickaxe

Voidry. A work- or clothes-basket, a voider.

Voore. A furrow made by a plough.

Voyer. The head land round a field

Vugg. Holes in a mineral vein in which valuable specimens are often found.

Vurden. A farthing.

W

Waiter. A tea tray.

Wallage. A bundle.

Want. A mole.

Want-hill A mole-hill.

Waps. The gadfly.

Warra. A pulley.

Warn. To warrant.

Way. Reason. "The way I called was to stop you."

Wazygoose. A printer's bean feast ; a contrivance for frightening birds from fruit trees—a "whizabout."

Ween. To chirp or cry plaintively.

Wees. Small gentry, people of great pretensions and little qualifications.

Weggas. The bindweed.

Werraking. Swinging a thing clumsily.

Werratting. Annoying, teasing, worrying.

Wheal. A mine.

Whilk. A stye.

Whiddles. Whims, fancies.

Whiff. To fish with lines towing after the boat.

Whirl. The hip joint.

Whistercuff. A blow, a box on the ear.

Whitear. The gristle in meat.

White witch. A fortune-teller, a quack; also a poor-tempered person.

Whitneck. A stoat, a weasel. "Screech like a whitneck."

Whiz. To throw quickly; a blow.

Whizabout. A whirligig.

Widdle. To wriggle, to squirm.

Widow-man. A widower.

Widow-woman. A widow.

Wiff. A cape.

Wiffle-headed. Thoughtless. "Our boy Bill, wiffle-headed and prodigal like, 'e would have two shirts."

Wildfire. The erysipelas (St. Anthony's fire). "Spread like wildfire."

Winding. Winnowing.

Windle. A windlass. "Windle of the pump."

Windspur. The roof at the gable of a house.

Windy. To winnow.

Winky-eye. A game played by hitting rotten eggs with a stick whilst blindfolded.

Winnard. The redwing.

Winnick. To cheat, to take in, to deceive.

Wisht. Melancholy, sad; to look ill. (Probably derived from the idea of "ill-wishing.")

Wod. A blow.

Woddle. A quantity of weak liquid; the dashing of water in a vessel.

Wog. To walk with a heavy, rolling motion.

Wonders. Frost bites, or stinging sensations caused by cold in the fingers.

Wood-tin. Tin ore, strongly resembling wood.

Wrinkle. The periwinkle.

Y

Yaffer. Heifer.

Yaffle. A loose armful; to pull about.

Yam. To eat greedily.

Yellow-janders. The jaundice.

Yewe. A farming implement, a dung fork.

Yuck. A yoke.—Formerly "breachy" pigs had frames of wood, called yokes, fixed round their necks to prevent their climbing fences.

Z

.

Zye. A scythe.

Zawn. A sea cavern. "Sawan" in *Williams'* Dictionary "a hole in the cliff through which the sea passeth;" and "Sawarn" is "a smell." Sea caverns have often an offensive smell from decaying weed or other matter in them.

LIST OF SUBSCRIBERS.

	COPIES.
Baker, W. K , *Towednack*	1
Bazeley, G P , *Penzance*	1
Beare, Mrs., *Penzance*	1
Beare, J. H., *Penzance*...	1
Bellows, John, *Gloucester*	1
Bickford, Mrs. J , *Camborne*.	4
Bickford, J. Vivian, *Camborne*	4
Bickford-Smith, W , *Helston*	1
Blanchford, Miss L , *Exeter*	1
Burgess, Dr. C.Venning, *Lond.*	1
Burrow, J. C., *Camborne* ..	1
Carbis, R , *Longrock* ..	1
Carter, Joseph J , *Elizabeth Penna, U.S.A.*	2
Chandler, W., *London* .	1
Clease, J., *Bristol* .	1
Code, Mrs , *The Rookery, Marazion* ..	2
Colenso, R., *Penzance*	1
Cornish, J. M., *Penzance*	1
Courtenay, Rt. Hon Leonard, *London*	1
Cox, Rev. J T., *Middlesboro'*	1
Craze, F., *Lelant*	1
Cunnack, R. J., *Illogan*	1
Dale, C F., *Penzance*	1
Dale, W., *Helston* .	4

	COPIES.
Drew, S. K., *Liverpool* . . .	1
Dunstan, J P, *St. Columb* ..	1
Edmonds, Mrs. M , *Marazion*	1
Endean, W., *Falmouth*	2
Enys, John D , *Penryn*	1
Eslick, Capt. Jos., *Scorrier* . .	1
Field, Thos. W., *Marazion* ..	2
Fox, Robert, *Falmouth*	1
Freeman, James, *Gunwalloe* ...	1
Gartrell, Mrs., *Paul*	5
Gartrell, J. H., *Penzance* ..	1
Gilbart, James, *Hayle*	1
Gillard, S., *St. Austell*	1
Goldsworthy, W. S , *London*	1
Hartley, Rev. J., *Middlesboro'*	2
Hawken, Miss E., *London* ...	1
Hellyar, R , *St. Columb*	1
Hendy, Ira, *Fremington* .. .	1
Hendy, John, *Grantham* ...	3
Hendy, W. J., *Trinidad* ...	2
Hendy, S., *Gunwalloe*	1
Hicks, Thomas, *St. Columb* ..	1
Hocken, Canon, *Hayle*	1
Holman, N., *St. Just* ...	6
Holman, F., *Penzance*	2
Hosken, W., *Hayle* ..	1
Jago, T. F., *Marazion* ..	1

138

COPIES.   COPIES.

James, Miss A., *Perranwell* .. 1

James, J., *Perranwell* 1

James, J. Hermanan, *Swansea* 1

Johns, H., *Johannesburg* . 1

Johns, W. J., *Marazion* ... 1

Kirsop, Rev. J., *Penzance* .. 1

Laity, R. Cornish, *Marazion* 3

Laity, H., *Sennen* 1

Lambrick, J. T., *St. Martin* . 1

Layland, Rev. J. J. H.,   *Wednesbury* ... 1

Lean, Thomas, *Marazion* .. 4

Lee, Mrs C. J., *London* . 4

Lethby, J., *Penzance* . . 1

Lory, James, *Cury* 2

Lowry, H. D., *London* 2

Luff, H. G., *Devonport* 1

Luke, Rev. W., *Marazion* ... 1

Manners, Capt. C., *Grenadier Guards* .. 1

Matthews, Miss, *Mullion* ... 1

Matthews, J., *London* . 1

Matthews, W., *London* 1

Matson, Miss S. A., *Brentwood* 4

Millett, Mrs. J., *London* .. 1

Millett, Fortescue W., *Marazion* ... 1

Mitchell, E., *Lelant* 1

Mitchell, F. W., *Penzance* . 1

Moore, J. G. D., *Grampound Road* . 3

Morgan, J. R , *St. Erth* ... 2

Mount-Edgcumbe, the Earl of, *Mount-Edgcumbe* ... 1

Nicholl, John, *Redruth* ... 1

Nickell, George, *Helland* ... 2

Newall, J. D. S., *Penzance* .. 1

Opie, James, *Penzance* 1

Parker, J., & Co., *Oxford* ... 2

Pearce, G. B., *Hayle* 1

Pearce, Vivian, *Hayle* 1

Pengelly, J. W., *Penzance* ... 1

Perry, W. T. L., *Penzance* ... 1

Peter, Thurstan C., *Redruth*... 1

Phillips Bros., *Marazion* ... 3

Polkinghorn, S. J., *Truro* ... 1

Polwhele, T. R., *Polwhele, Truro* 2

Preston, R. H., *Penzance* ... 1

Rawling, J., *Launceston* ... 1

Robinson, G. P. A., *Penzance* 2

Rodda, J. S., *Pendeen* 1

Rodda, W. H., *San Francisco* 1

Rogers, M., *Johannesburg* ... 1

Rundle, Rev. S., *Helston* ... 1

St. Aubyn, Molesworth, *Clowance* ... 2

St. Levan, the Lord, *St. Michael's Mount* ... 8

Saundry, Miss, *Penzance* ... 1

Shapcote, C. A., *Devonport* ... 1

Smales, W. C.. *Ludgvan* ... 1

Smith, J., *Penzance* 2

Titley, John, *Gloucester* ... 1

Thomas, Mrs. E., *Mullion* ... 3

Thomas, George, *Penzance* ... 1

Thomas, John, *Mullion* 3

Thomas, Joseph, *Mullion* ... 1

	COPIES.
Thomas, R., *Mullion* .	1
Thomas, W. Henry, *London* .	6
Thomas, W. Hendy, *Mullion*	1
Thomas, W. Herbert, *Penzance*	1
Tonkin, Miss C., *Mullion* .	1
Tonking, Richd. H., *Greenwich*	1
Thornley, Rev J , *Sheffield* .	1
Toy, H., *Helston*	2
Trebilcock, Mrs., *Penzance*	1
Tregelles, G. F., *Barnstaple* .	2
Treglown, J., *Marazion*	1
Trevaskis, J., *Penzance* ...	2
Trewecke, F., *Oxford*	3
Trounson, E., *Redruth* .. .	1
Trounson, T., *Redruth* . .	1

	COPIES.
Tucker, Edmund, *St. Germans*	1
Uren, Charles H., *Penzance* .	1
Victor, H , *Penzance*	1
Vinter, H. W., *Truro*	2
Vivian, H. Phillips, *Camborne*	1
Webster, A., & Co.. *London* .	1
White, W. T., *Heamoor* ..	1
White, Miss, *Rosecadyhill* ...	1
Williams, Mrs., *St. Just* ...	1
Williams, J., *Marazion*	1
Williams, J. M., *London* ..	1
Williams, Peter, *Helston* .	1
Willis, Edward, *Devonport* ...	6
Wright, F. A., *Penzance* .	1

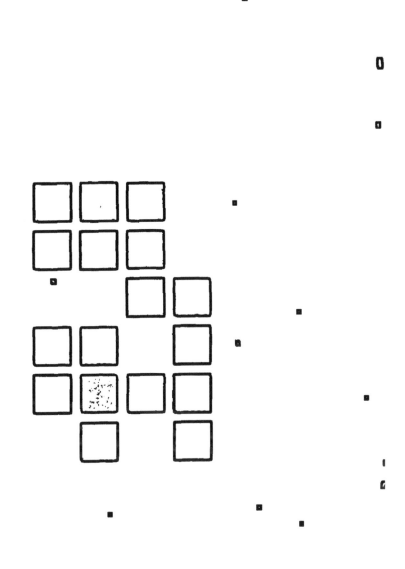

Lightning Source UK Ltd.
Milton Keynes UK
UKHW021127300522
403723UK00006B/1713